# Your Pregnancy and Newborn Journey

# Your Pregnancy and Newborn Journey
## A Guide for Pregnant Teens

Jeanne Warren Lindsay, MA, CFCS
and
Jean Brunelli, PHN

Morning Glory Press

Buena Park, California

*Your Pregnancy and Newborn Journey*

is part of a six-book series. Other titles are:

*Nurturing Your Newborn*

*Your Baby's First Year*

*The Challenge of Toddlers*

*Discipline from Birth to Three*

*Teen Dads: Rights, Responsibilities and Joys*

Library of Congress Cataloging-in-Publication Data
Lindsay, Jeanne Warren.
    Your pregnancy and newborn journey : a guide for pregnant teens /
Jeanne Warren Lindsay and Jean Brunelli.
        p.    cm. -- (Teens parenting)
    Includes bibliographical references and index.
    Summary: Discusses nutritional, medical, and social aspects of
teenage pregnancy and teenage parenthood.
    ISBN 1-932538-01-1 (hbk.). -- ISBN 1-932538-00-3 (pbk.)
    1. Prenatal care--Juvenile literature.    2. Teenage pregnancy--
Juvenile literature.    3. Teenage parents--Juvenile literature.
(1. Pregnancy.    2. Teenage parents. ]    I. Brunelli, Jean, 1934-    .
II. Title.    III. Series: Lindsay, Jeanne Warren.    Teens parenting.
RG556.5.L564   1998
618.2'4'0835--dc21                                                98-7616
                                                                         CIP
                                                                          AC

MORNING GLORY PRESS, INC.
6595 San Haroldo Way     Buena Park, CA 90620-3748
714/828-1998    1/888-612-8254
Printed and bound in the United States of America

# Contents

# Acknowledgments

Most important to us is the input from pregnant and parenting teens, the young people we interviewed, and whose wisdom is scattered throughout the book. Sixty-one young people were quoted in the 1991 edition. In 1998, we interviewed 54 additional pregnant and parenting teens, and in 2003, additional teens. Many gave us permission to include their names.

Those interviewed in 1998 and 2003 and quoted in this book include Maria Negrete, Gladys Medina, Sonia Leandro, Alysson Hall, Allen Cain, Carlos Smith, Andrea Gonzales, Angelina Rojas, Caroline Quintero, Cecilia Diaz, Danielle Alston, Jason Banks, Janelle Byers, Jill Winkler, Jessica Marquez, Katrina Amaya, Larry Vargas, Francis Hernandez, Laura Lilio, Maria Almarez, Nicole Perez, Rosa Paez, Tiffany Torres, Tina Mondragon, Yvette Aguirre, Antonee Williams, and Monica Gandara, Others are quoted and acknowledged in the other books in the *Teens Parenting* series. We also appreciate the many other teenage parents whose insightful quotes are retained from the earlier edition.

The late David Crawford, teacher in the Teen Mother Program, William Daylor High School, Sacramento, supplied most of the earlier photographs, and Carole Blum was the photographer for this edition. Their models were teen parent students. Jami Moffett and Barbara Hellstrom provided the illustrations.

Tim Rinker is the cover artist, and Steve Lindsay helped design the book. We appreciate so much the contributions of all of these talented people.

Karen Blake again helped with the proof-reading and kept Morning Glory Press alive and well during book production time. We thank her for her valuable support.

We're especially grateful to our ever-supportive spouses, Mike Brunelli and Bob Lindsay. We love them.

*Jeanne Lindsay*                                                           *Jean Brunelli*

# Preface

If you're going to have a baby, you're preparing for a wonderful and sometimes scary event. Your baby's healthy development depends to a great extent on what you do throughout your pregnancy. Your own health and well-being depend on you taking good care of yourself during this important time.

This book is for you. It's not written for your teachers or your parents or for students in your school's health class. It's written directly to you, a pregnant teenager, and to your partner if you're still together.

Much of *Your Pregnancy and Newborn Journey* focuses on your pregnancy and on your labor and delivery. Your baby will become more and more real to you as the months go by, and how you care for yourself is extremely important to that small person inside you.

As you do all you can to help your baby develop well, remember that your needs continue to be extremely important. You're a teenager who happens to be pregnant. You have a lot of decisions to make and planning to do regarding your coming child. Don't forget your own needs as you do this planning.

We have both worked with hundreds of pregnant teenagers, and for this book we interviewed in depth many of these young women. We've also interviewed teenage fathers because we thought you'd be interested in their feelings on the subject of their fatherhood.

Actually, this book is co-authored not just by us, but also by these many young people who shared their experiences and their thoughts with us. As each young parent is quoted, s/he is identified by age, children, and children's ages. If the same parent is quoted again in the same chapter, only her/his name is listed. Names have been changed, but the quotes and the ages given are always real.

These young parents discuss their reasons for eating nutritious foods and staying away from alcohol, drugs, and smoking during pregnancy. They share their labor and delivery stories. They talk about the stresses and the joys of caring for a newborn baby. You may find their comments more helpful than ours because these are your peers, young people who have already experienced the things you're experiencing as a pregnant teen.

We wish you the best as you continue on your pregnancy and newborn journey — surely one of the most important journeys you will ever take.

Jeanne Lindsay
Jean Brunelli
August, 2003

# Foreword

Nearly half a million young women have babies each year in the United States. Many of these adolescents do not realize the health risks involved in having a child at such a young age. They have undertaken the task of developing another human being while their own bodies are still developing. The birth of premature/low birthweight infants is associated with inadequate prenatal care. This is the leading cause of death in the first month of a child's life.

Low birthweight is a largely solvable problem. We know a great deal about what causes it, and how to prevent it. It is vitally important that pregnant teens receive early and adequate prenatal care. Today we know the importance of detecting and preventing problems, such as lifestyle, genetic, and environmental, that can affect the baby at every stage of development.

I have been involved with pregnant adolescents through the March of Dimes Birth Defects Foundation's interest in the alarming statistics of babies delivered to these mothers, statistics concerning both low-birthweight and birth defects, and then determining how to improve those statistics. At the March of Dimes, experience has shown that the first step in preventing birth defects is to minimize risk. The first step in minimizing risk is education!

A pregnant teen who continues her education has a decided advantage both physically and emotionally. Support in the school setting has proven to be a key factor in improved pregnancy outcome. There, she becomes aware of her responsibility in keeping prenatal care appointments and maintaining a healthy diet. She learns how important it is to avoid smoking, alcohol, and drugs because all are added risks to her developing baby.

Jeanne Lindsay and Jean Brunelli's book is an important tool in education. As usual, Jeanne's interviews with pregnant and parenting teens are lessons in reality.

Working with thousands of teen parents over the past thirty years has given Jeanne and Jean insight in and sensitivity to the needs of this special population.

Life's most important journey is usually a stunning success — *if* the baby's parents are making healthy choices to achieve this goal. *Your Pregnancy and Newborn Journey* is a very special, readable, and practical book.

Anita A. Gallegos
Former Director, Community Services
March of Dimes Birth Defects Foundation
Southern California Chapter

To our students
who helped us develop the knowledge
we share here

*They're already parenting their unborn children.*

# 1

# Parenting Starts With Pregnancy

*I really didn't want to grow up. I didn't want to be a mom. I wanted to go out. I wasn't planning to have the baby. I was already at the clinic to have an abortion, but they said I was too far along. I'm happy now that I'm having it.*

Anneliese, 17 - 8 months pregnant

*I was real sad because I couldn't believe I was pregnant — and I didn't want to believe it. But as I got bigger and bigger, I finally had to face it. I had to move on to the next step.*

*My parents were hurt, but they stuck by me and helped me deal with the situation.*

Elysha, pregnant at 17

*When I first started showing, I was afraid to go out in
public because I was ashamed of myself. I didn't want
anything to do with being pregnant, but it's a fact of life.*

Liz, pregnant at 15

This book is about pregnancy. It's also about parenting
because parenting begins at conception. How you take care
of yourself while you're pregnant is an extremely important
part of parenting. What you do now has a great deal to do
with your baby becoming a mentally and physically healthy
human being.

*I encouraged Ynez to eat during pregnancy. It's
about her and the baby, not about us.*

Del, 20, partner of Ynez, pregnant at 15

If you see your healthcare provider regularly, eat the
"right" foods, and avoid alcohol, tobacco, and drugs, you're
being a "good" parent long before you can hold your baby
in your arms.

> **Early Signs of Pregnancy**
> • Period is one week or more late.
> • Extreme sleepiness
> • Tender breasts
> • Upset stomach, sometimes with vomiting

A baby can be most damaged during the first three
months of pregnancy. Many women don't see a doctor and
may not know they're pregnant during this important time.

Since you're reading this book, you've probably already
verified your pregnancy. You and your partner may be
pleased and excited about your coming baby. Perhaps your
family is supportive, too.

## Your Feelings Matter

How are you feeling about yourself? Some teens are excited about being pregnant. Having a new life growing inside you can be exciting.

*When I first realized I was pregnant, it was okay. I was living with my boyfriend and his parents, and we planned having a baby.*

Emmy, pregnant at 17

If this pregnancy came as a shock to you, however, you may be feeling pretty depressed about the whole thing.

*I stopped going to my regular high school when I was three months pregnant. I didn't want anybody to know, so I didn't go anywhere. I think that made everything worse. I could have stayed at my regular high school and gone ahead with my activities at least for awhile.*

Maurine, pregnant at 14

Many pregnant teens are frightened and even a little desperate when they realize they're pregnant "too soon." If this is how you feel, you need to find help immediately. Can you talk to a school nurse, guidance counselor, or your healthcare provider? Or you might start with your priest, rabbi, minister, imam, or other spiritual leader.

## See Your Healthcare Provider Early!

How do you know you're pregnant? You've probably missed a period. Your breasts may already be getting bigger. Perhaps you're throwing up in the mornings. You may be feeling crankier than usual.

Whatever your symptoms, if you think you're pregnant, please see a health professional right away. Get your questions answered. You may be scared — the unknown is often *very* scary. Perhaps you don't know what to do.

You could start by buying a home pregnancy test kit. (*Ovulation* test kits are often displayed next to the pregnancy test kits. Be sure you choose the *pregnancy* test kit.) They can be used on the first day that your period is late. Follow the directions carefully. If you test positive, the best thing to do now is to find a clinic where you can get your home test results verified.

As you probably realize by now, trying to pretend you aren't pregnant won't help anyone. Yet many young women, shocked at the idea of having conceived, ignore the whole thing — sometimes for several months.

> *I ignored the whole idea of pregnancy for six or seven months. I didn't tell my parents until right before I enrolled in the Teen Parent Program. I ignored it for the whole summer.*
>
> *My boyfriend had moved, so it was just me. He moved before I found out I was pregnant, so I didn't tell him. He still doesn't know.*
>
> Pati, pregnant at 16

Getting your pregnancy verified early is important for several reasons. First, a lot of young women who don't want to be pregnant go through the agony of thinking they are, when, in fact, they aren't. If you aren't pregnant, you might as well find out. Then, if you don't want to be pregnant, you and your partner can either not have sex or one or both of you can use contraception.

You'll have less chance of conceiving and/or contracting an STI (sexually transmitted infection) if he uses a condom *and* you also use a method such as taking the birth control pill every day, using the contraceptive patch, or getting a birth control injection (such as Depo Provera) every three months. See chapter 12 for more on birth control.

Incidentally, some STIs can harm your baby if you're

not treated early in pregnancy, and might cause birth defects.

Second, you have more options if your pregnancy is verified early. If you consider having an abortion, you need to make your decision as soon as possible. An abortion performed very early in pregnancy, preferably during the first twelve weeks after conception, is easier on the woman both physically and emotionally than is a later abortion. Seldom will an abortion be performed on a person who is more than twenty weeks pregnant. If you're having trouble deciding what to do, talk to a counselor or healthcare provider.

*For six months I didn't show, I didn't gain weight, and I just didn't think about it. I blocked it out of my mind. Then all of a sudden, I had an ultrasound done, and I was 26 weeks pregnant.*

*Of course that was too far along to do anything except keep it. I didn't really realize I couldn't have an abortion until the counselor said, "Well, it's too late now."*

Lucia, 16 - placed her baby for adoption

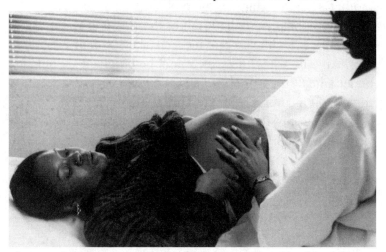

*Let your healthcare provider guide you to a safe and healthy delivery.*

Third, and perhaps the most important reason for an early pregnancy test, is the need for early and regular prenatal care throughout pregnancy. If you're pregnant, you need to see your healthcare provider right away. ("Healthcare provider" may be a doctor, midwife, nurse practitioner, or physician's assistant.)

*If I had told my grandmother sooner, I probably would have gotten prenatal care. I think it would have helped me both mentally and physically. Hiding was hard. I was nervous, always tense, never wanted to come home because I didn't want them to see me. Everyone was getting the idea, and I wanted to be the one to tell my grandma.*

*I guess I waited so long because I was scared. I thought my boyfriend was going to be there through everything to help me, but he wasn't. It doesn't always work out the way you want it to.*

Elisa Marie, pregnant at 14

*Early* prenatal care is essential for baby's as well as mother's health. Many of the problems teenagers face during pregnancy are the result of these young women not seeing their healthcare provider until late in their pregnancies. Anyone who thinks she might be pregnant should be under a healthcare provider's care at least by the time she's three months pregnant, preferably sooner.

The health professional will check you carefully for any condition which might interfere with a healthy pregnancy. She will probably prescribe prenatal vitamins and recommend the kinds of foods you should be eating.

## Pelvic Examination

On your first visit and again toward the end of your pregnancy, the doctor will do a "pelvic" examination.

You'll be asked to undress and put on a hospital gown. During the examination you'll be lying on your back with your knees bent and your feet in stirrups (metal things on the end of the table to hold your feet out of the way). Your body will be covered with a sheet from the waist down.

The doctor will put on gloves and place a finger in your vagina while s/he presses on your stomach. Next, while seated, the doctor will look in your vagina. To see well, an instrument (speculum) will be put in your vagina to hold it open. (This does not hurt.)

By looking and feeling, the doctor can see physical signs of pregnancy, signs of infection, and obtain other helpful information.

## Medical Expenses of Pregnancy

Important as it is, medical care during pregnancy and delivery is expensive. A pregnant teenager may qualify for medical care under her family's health plan. Or she and/or her baby's father may have health insurance through work.

In some states, if you don't have health insurance, you may be eligible for Medicaid during pregnancy and for your child after s/he is born.

If you are covered, you can get prenatal health care at no charge to you or to your parents. To find out if this is available where you live, ask a social worker at school or in your health care agency, or call the local Department of Public Social Services (welfare department). Some areas have prenatal health clinics where women can get prenatal checkups at no charge — or they may be charged according to their income.

In many states, however, parents are not covered by Medicaid. Find out what is available in your state.

Many organizations such as the March of Dimes Birth Defects Foundation are concerned about the poor outcome

of many teenage pregnancies. They know that teenagers
who do not get early medical care are more likely to have
serious health problems themselves during pregnancy.
They also know that babies born to teenage mothers may be
born too soon and be smaller than average. Premature, too-
small babies are more likely to have physical and mental
handicaps than are bigger, full-term babies.

For these reasons, the March of Dimes especially wants
to help pregnant teenagers get good prenatal care. If you
don't know where to go or how to pay for such care, contact your local March of Dimes office. They may be able to
help you locate the community resources you need.

## Healthcare Providers for Pregnant Women

- **Family doctor** provides prenatal care; delivers
  babies vaginally; refers unusual cases to specialists;
  usually delivers in hospitals only.
- **Obstetrician** provides prenatal care, delivers
  babies at hospitals and/or birthing centers; does
  both vaginal and cesarean deliveries.
- **Midwife** is a trained medical person (not a doctor)
  who assists with birth in hospital or birthing center.

The important point is that when you are pregnant, no
matter how old you are, you see your healthcare provider
early and regularly for care.

## Stay in School!

*If there's anything I learned through this whole
thing that I wish I could change is that I'd have stayed
in school. Like this year I should be graduating with
my class. I got pregnant as a freshman in high school,
and I dropped out soon after.*

Leila, 18 - Larissa, 21/2

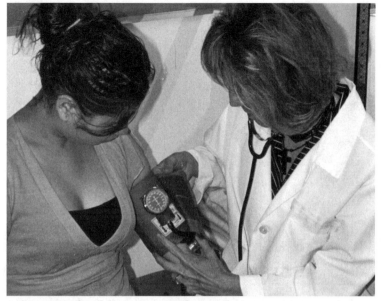

*See your health care provider early in your pregnancy.*

A generation or two ago, pregnant teens were not allowed to attend school. What a strange system it was to push a person out of school *because* she was to become a parent. It's even more important that you continue your education if you'll be caring for and teaching your child.

You're also likely to need job skills to support your child whether or not you're with your baby's father. Even if you're together, or if he provides child support, you're still likely to work. Chances are you'll want to earn money to help pay for all the things your child will need.

Government supports such as TANF (Temporary Aid to Needy Families) now helps families only for a brief period of time. Anyone receiving TANF grants needs to be preparing to be self sufficient. This also applies to pregnant teens.

Continuing your education, planning for your career, and learning job skills are especially crucial if you're going to have a baby.

*I would have liked to stay home while I was preg-
nant, but I had come this far, and I was determined to
graduate with my class.*

*Those who drop out because of pregnancy miss out.
They think, "I have a baby so I can't graduate." They
can do it if they really want to.*

*You don't have to have a negative attitude about it.
The highlight of the senior year is being able to look
at your friends and say, "Gosh, we did it. We did it
together." You can still do that if you're pregnant.*

Elysha

In some states (California and others) financial aid
(TANF) is offered only to teen parents in school or job
training full-time. Even then, there are limits on how long
a person remains eligible for aid.

Is there a special school program in your area for pregnant and parenting teens? Public high schools and some
private schools can no longer legally push students out of
regular classes because of pregnancy or marital status.
Neither can they require students to attend a special
program for pregnant and parenting teens.

However, if there is a special program, you'd probably
take prenatal health and parenting classes there. You'd also
be more likely to get help in solving any problems you may
have because of your pregnancy.

Many pregnant teens have talked to us about the benefits
of being with other teens with experiences similar to theirs:

*You learn how to stay healthy, eat the right foods,
learn what to expect before you go into labor and
after. The girls that don't come here, it's because they
don't want to really believe they're pregnant.*

*When you come here it has to kick in. You're
pregnant, and what are you going to do after you*

*have the baby? Are you going to work? Going to
college? I've learned a lot here.*

Marlee, 18 - 6 months pregnant

More and more, teen parent programs are encouraging
fathers to attend along with mothers. Young fathers often
need special help, too.

Even if you haven't started high school yet, hang in
there. You can still work toward high school graduation
while you're pregnant and after you have your baby. Both
you and your baby will be glad you did.

Pregnancy is *not* a disease. One of the most important
things you can do for yourself and your child is to *stay in
school.* Remember, if you're attending public school, you
have a right to be there throughout your pregnancy. You
can return as soon after delivery as you feel able.

If you're in a private school, you may want to check
with your counselor or your principal. If you find you want
or are asked to leave that school, be sure you transfer to
either a special program for pregnant teens or your local
public school. To repeat, *don't drop out of school!*

## Your Parents' Reaction

*I was scared, shocked, in denial. I didn't want to
believe I was pregnant. My mom cried. She couldn't
believe her little girl was pregnant. My dad was real
mad. He still doesn't talk to me to this day. I try to
talk to him but I can't force things.*

Anneliese

Some teens find it extremely difficult to tell their parents
about their pregnancy. Perhaps their parents have told their
daughter she would have to leave home if she got pregnant
too soon, or said to their son that he must move out if he
caused a pregnancy.

Parents of pregnant teens react in many different ways. Most are shocked, many are unhappy, and some blame themselves for "allowing" this to happen. In fact, many parents of pregnant teens experience real grief about a pregnancy which, they feel, will take away their daughter's or their son's childhood. After a short time, most parents tend to be supportive of their teens' needs.

> *At first Dad cried. He said I was too young, and I should think about abortion. I told him I couldn't do that because I would always wonder. My mom seemed sort of happy. She was going to be a grandmother.*
>
> Carla, pregnant at 16

Some parents take a long time to get over their shock, as was the case with Christina's family:

> *When the nurse told me I was pregnant, I went over to my sister's house. She called my aunt, and my aunt told my mom I was pregnant. My mom got furious. All my sisters were mad at me already. My mom called me at my sister's, and she started screaming at me. "Why did you do that?" She had trusted me. I knew I was wrong in getting pregnant, but I couldn't tell her anything because she was already so mad at me. Everybody was angry, and nobody talked to me.*
>
> *I moved in with my sister, and she took me to the clinic when I was three or four months along. I stayed with her for four months. I only saw my parents once or twice during that time. They didn't really want to see me then, but I came back home in June. It's working pretty well.*
>
> Christina, pregnant at 15

Coming from a culture different from that of most of your friends can make things harder. If your parents grew up with quite different customs than those in your neighborhood, they may find it even more difficult to accept your pregnancy. Lei was 11 when she moved to the United States with her family. She explained:

> *In my country you don't even get a boyfriend until you're in college and you're at least 20. They think you're a little kid until you're 25. My brother was 17 when he had his first girlfriend, and my parents thought it was too early.*
>
> *I got tired of them because they didn't give me a chance to grow up. They said I couldn't go out with guys until I was 21. I couldn't even go out with a guy who was just a friend.*
>
> *I left when I was 16 and moved in with my boyfriend. Then I got pregnant. They said I could come home if I'd get an abortion. They said they would forgive me, and that we would talk about it. I knew the same thing was going to happen, that they wouldn't let me see my boyfriend. It was a battle. They say they hear what I say, but they don't really think about it.*
>
> *They called me a lot at my boyfriend's house, and it was real hard. Later my aunt talked to my mom and said, "She's your only daughter and you have to help her." So my mother asked us to move back. We didn't really want to, but we did because we needed to save money for the baby. We got married, and we moved back. My dad still doesn't accept us very well.*
>
> Lei, pregnant at 16

If cultural differences are making it extra hard for you and your parents, try to talk with them. Try to understand their point of view, and attempt to work out a plan that will work for all of you.

If you aren't happy about this pregnancy and you don't

feel you're ready to be a parent, you may want to consider
other alternatives. If you decide to continue your pregnancy, you can also consider an adoption plan.

In fact, it's a good idea to make a parenting plan *and* an
adoption plan. Then you can look at the good things and the
not-so-good things about each plan as you make your
decision. For more information on the very difficult choice
of adoption, see chapter 6, "For Some, Adoption Is
an Option."

## Mother/Daughter Relationship

Sometimes a pregnant teen reports that she feels closer
to her mother than she did before. Perhaps the crisis of the
pregnancy helped both mother and daughter forget some of
their past differences. Perhaps her mother feels needed
again by her daughter. Or for some, it's simply the excitement of the coming grandchild. Miranda was only 13 when
she conceived. She commented:

> *My mom was disappointed when she found out I*
> *was pregnant. The pregnancy changed our relation-*
> *ship. I didn't used to tell her things. I didn't talk to*
> *her much because I didn't care. Now I tell her stuff,*
> *how I feel, what I'm doing. We've gotten closer.*
>
> Miranda, pregnant at 13

Coping with their teenage daughter's pregnancy is hard
for many parents. If this is the case in your family, try to
understand your family's feelings. If you share some of
the things you're feeling, they may be a little more
understanding.

Perhaps family counseling would help. If you are attached to a religious community, ask your pastor, priest,
imam, rabbi, or other religious advisor for suggestions as to
where to find counseling. Or you could call Family

Services for help. Many hospitals and some schools also have support groups for parents.

## Your Partner's Reaction

*When I got pregnant, it was exciting, but scary, too. I was very much still my mama's baby. I told my boyfriend who had joined the Army a couple of weeks earlier.*

*I had thought he would be upset, but he seemed to be fine. He kept telling me he wanted to get married. I wanted to be sure he wasn't marrying me just because I was pregnant.*

*We didn't see each other until that Christmas when I was already showing, and he was excited. We got married while he was home. We haven't really lived together yet.*

Dawn Ellen, pregnant at 17

*Their pregnancy makes big changes in both their lives.*

How is your baby's father reacting to your pregnancy? Becoming a father earlier than he expected can be pretty scary. If you're still with your baby's father, are you considering marriage? Or perhaps you're already married.

Thirty years ago, marriage was considered the answer to too-early pregnancy. If the young man didn't want to marry the young woman he'd gotten pregnant, her father was likely to demand that he do so. Sometimes the couple moved on to many years of happiness together.

For many other couples, it didn't work. Teenagers change rapidly as they develop. The interests they had at 16 may be far removed from the interests each will have at age 22.

The couple married at 16 may find themselves to be two very different people by the time they're 20. In fact, if the partners in a marriage aren't yet 18, their marriage is four times as likely to fail within a few years as is a marriage between people in their 20s.

> *We got a little apartment, and that was hard. He was working construction. We had only one room in that first apartment, but it was nice.*
>
> *I was scared because I was away from home. You see, I was always close to my mom. It was exciting, but it was also scary to be out on my own. After we had Francene it was nice, but being a mother is hard.*
>
> Joanne, pregnant at 18

## If He's Not with You

Sometimes one's partner seems to change when he learns she's pregnant:

> *We found out I was pregnant when I was three months. It was weird. I didn't know if I should be happy or sad. I kind of laughed and cried at the same time.*

*I'm with the father sort of, but he's changed a lot.*

Anessa, pregnant at 17

If you aren't with your baby's father, you still have decisions to make. Will you put his name on your baby's birth certificate? Will you file for child support? You probably should.

While you might prefer to pretend this man has nothing to do with your baby, it's your baby's needs that you must respect. It really isn't fair to your child not to have the father help support him, both emotionally and financially.

## Safety for Mom and Baby

Usually it's better for a child to know his father. If both parents live and parent together, great. If they aren't together, both can still parent their child. A child who doesn't know one of his parents is likely to feel abandoned by that parent.

If you are in an abusive relationship with your baby's father, however, you need to make it clear that either the abuse stops or you split. Eight to ten percent of pregnant women in the United States are physically abused by their partners during pregnancy, some for the first time. This may result in a low birthweight, premature baby, and, rarely, infant death.

At all times, but especially during pregnancy it is important for both mother and her developing baby to feel safe. Pregnant women who experience abuse during their pregnancy have emotional and physical responses that may cause their baby to develop less well. The hormones secreted during periods of anxiety reach the baby's blood supply. This can cause the baby to experience increased restless movement and slower weight gain.

Babies who have these experiences are sometimes born

prematurely, have difficulty attaching to their parent, and
may be either very fussy or exceptionally quiet and
watchful.

If you do not have a safe place to be while you're pregnant, call the National Domestic Violence Hot Line,
800.799.7233. A trained counselor will help you.

The birth of the child almost never makes the problem
go away. When a baby witnesses abuse, s/he is affected by
it in many ways. Both you and your baby need to be in a
safe place.

If your partner is abusing you, it's not likely to get better
over time. If you aren't living with him, it probably would
be easier to break away than if you were living together and
you had no place else to go. Either way, if you need help
with this problem, call a local women's shelter or the Hot
Line listed above.

## Gangs and Pregnancy

Violence is often a part of gang involvement. If you're in
a gang, do you think you and your baby are safe?

*I stopped messing around with gangs when I got
pregnant with my daughter. I thought, they aren't
going to help me with my daughter. I still see my
homeboys and homegirls, but it's not like seeing them
every day. I'd like nobody to get into gangs.*

*It's not worth it. They aren't going to help you
support your kid, and if you die, they won't take your
kid. It's hard in a gang because they make you do
stupid stuff. I just left, no turning back. They disown
you, but it's not real dangerous in my area.*

Bridget, 18 - Caelin 21/2; Barnaby, 6 months

In some areas, walking away from a gang is far more
dangerous than it was for Bridget. Sometimes a young

person must move to an entirely different area to be free of the gang influence s/he no longer wants. Sometimes it's important to take such an extreme measure. After all, it's your baby's well-being you're concerned about now.

## Life Goes On

*I'd had years and years of my parents telling me not to do this and not to do that, and it went in one ear and out the other. But when I got pregnant with Clancy, it was a wake-up call. It was like someone had shined a light on me and said, "Wake up, you need to grow up now. You can't go out and party every night," and I started to settle down.*

*I was frightened, but as time went on and I got used to the idea of being a mother, I calmed down. I realized I must be responsible for myself as well as another little human being.*

*I'm focusing on getting a career for myself and bringing him up the way I would have liked. I want him to have opportunities I didn't have.*

Chelsea, 19 - Clancy, 2 months

Whether you plan to parent your child yourself or are considering adoption, how you take care of yourself during these coming months matters a great deal. It's up to you to help your baby develop into a healthy newborn.

Some babies are born too small and too soon. If you eat the right foods, don't smoke, drink, or take drugs, and get good prenatal health care, your chances of producing a normal healthy baby are extremely good.

*What are you doing for your baby today?*

*For more information, see **Surviving Teen Pregnancy** by Shirley Arthur (Morning Glory Press).*

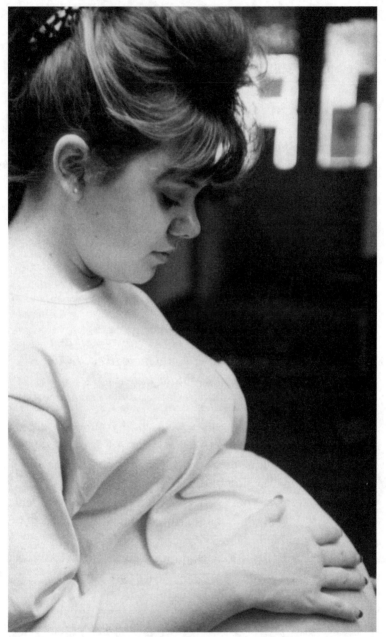

*Pregnancy brings changes to one's body.*

# 2

# Dealing with Minor Discomforts

- *Always* Tired
- Morning Sickness — All Day
- Where's the Bathroom?
- Are You Dizzy?
- Moodiness Strikes
- Heartburn
- Constipation
- Varicose Veins and Hemorrhoids
- If You Can't Sleep
- Backaches
- Movement — Baby
- Danger Signs
- Pregnancy Is n't Permanent

*I get real bad back pains, and I had a bladder infection and a bloody nose. It feels weird going through these changes because I was used to being so healthy. And gaining all this weight . . .*

Deborah, pregnant at 17

*I had morning sickness for five months. I lost 15 pounds in the beginning because I couldn't keep anything down, but I gained it back. The doctor told me just to eat a little bit at a time so I could try to keep it down. It was like certain smells, a lot of different things made me sick.*

Brooke, 18 - Blair, 3 months

Newly pregnant young women often comment that they're not used to feeling uncomfortable so often. Pregnancy brings changes in one's body, changes that are sometimes pleasant, sometimes unpleasant.

You can do something about some of these discomforts. First, remember that no one has ever been permanently pregnant — all these things will pass. In fact, some of them will change during your pregnancy.

*My first couple of months up to my fifth I had morning sickness. My sixth and seventh months were great.*

LaTisha, pregnant at 15

## *Always* **Tired**

*At first I was always tired and I was sleeping all day. I didn't know I was pregnant, and Chris kept saying, "You're pregnant, you're pregnant." Finally I admitted it.*

Erin, pregnant at 15

You may feel very tired during your first trimester (the first three months of your pregnancy). You might be so tired that you think you're sick and need to stay in bed.

*When I first moved in with Colin and his family, I got lazy. I quit going to cosmetology school. I could sleep 16 hours a day. I continued going to high school, but that was only 7:30-11. Then I'd go back to Colin's house, and I'd sleep the whole day.*

Chelsea, 19 - Clancy, 2 months

Actually, this tiredness is nature's way of helping your body shift gears and prepare for the development of your baby. The hormones shift, and your blood supply changes places slightly. Building a baby is a lot of work and makes you weary. This can be especially hard if you're working:

> *I'm working, and we only get ten minutes break for a five-hour shift. That's hard on me. Since I work at the cash register, I can't take a break if it's really busy, and I'm on my feet all the time. I go to school, and I get tired, so I cut back on my hours last week.*
>
> Libbey, 6 months pregnant

---

**Tired? Things you can do:**

• Take naps. Get more sleep at night.

• Change your position often.

• Figure out activities for which you must be alert. Do these things early in the day or right after you've had a nap.

• Exercise even when you feel tired. It really helps. Taking a walk after lunch or dinner may refresh you as much as a nap.

---

## Morning Sickness — All Day

> *I had morning sickness for three months. It was yukky. I couldn't stand up without feeling like I'd puke or pass out. I lost nearly 15 pounds. The doctor told me to eat crackers and water. I'd go to school, but I'd leave before lunch because the smell of the food would do me in.*
>
> Kellie, pregnant at 16

Nausea is probably the second most common discomfort of pregnancy. Many pregnant women feel sick first thing in the morning, so it's often called morning sickness. It can happen at any time of day, however. In fact, when I (Jean B.) was pregnant, I was most likely to be sick just before dinner. Since I did the cooking, this was especially hard.

Probably the worst thing you can do when you're feeling nauseous is *not* eat. The less you eat, the more nauseous or sick you'll get.

### Nausea? Things you can do:

• If you feel nauseous, try drinking lukewarm water or any lukewarm or cold liquid you like. Also try eating jello or popsicles.

• Salty snacks such as crackers sometimes help.

• Eating small meals more often may help. Don't worry too much about weight gain at this point. Concentrate on feeling better and eating from as many food groups as you can manage.

• Instead of frequent small meals, you might prefer to "graze" all day. During this stage, eat what appeals to you.

• Eating something before you go to bed may help you feel less sick.

• Be sure to check with your healthcare provider before you use over-the-counter medications to relieve nausea. Some of these medicines could harm your baby, but others are just fine.

• If you feel your vitamins are causing nausea, try taking them at different times of the day.

• Ask your doctor about an acupressure wrist bracelet.

## Where's the Bathroom?

As your uterus enlarges and your hormones shift, you'll probably have to urinate more often. This is normal early in pregnancy, and will be troublesome again during the last two or three months before your baby is born.

**If any of these things happen, call your doctor or go to the hospital emergency room:**

• If you have a burning sensation when you urinate.

• You feel you have to urinate, but little comes out.

• Urinating is painful.

These symptoms may indicate a bladder infection. Drinking liquids, especially cranberry juice, often helps. If you're nauseous, however, this may be difficult.

*I knew I was pregnant by two months. I was fine except for four or five bladder infections. Once I had it so bad I thought I was in labor. I'd go to the doctor and get medication each time. I hated the way I felt.*

Marsha, pregnant at 15

*If you feel dizzy, try this position.*

## Are You Dizzy?

Your blood supply changes as your rapidly growing uterus draws new circulation to the lower abdomen. As a result, you may sometimes feel dizzy, especially after you stand for a long time.

If this happens, lie down with your feet higher than your head. If you can't do that, sit down and put your head between your knees. Breathe as deeply as possible. If you feel dizzy toward the end of pregnancy, you'll probably have to lie down.

## Moodiness Strikes

*I don't even try to handle my emotions, not with everything going on with my boyfriend and my parents. Between stress and depression, I just try to get by. I'm scared about being a mother.*

Libbey

Do your moods change for no apparent reason? Do you find you're often crabby with your boyfriend or your little brother?

Think back to when you first began having periods. You may have had similar feelings because the hormones in your body were changing. Now those hormones are acting up even more as your body prepares for your coming baby. This in itself causes moodiness in many pregnant women.

You may have lots of things on your mind. So many decisions to make, so much to do. The reactions of your parents, your friends, your baby's father may not be what you'd like. You might call it mental overload.

*I was scared, I was embarrassed. I saw my sisters pregnant, and knew how they looked. I didn't want to look like that. I'd never been fat in my life. When I got pregnant, I thought, "Why do I have to gain so much weight? Why does my body have to change?"*

Meghan, pregnant at 17

Lots of people, when they realize they're about to become a mother, are scared or worried. If your boyfriend and/or your parents are less supportive than you'd like, of course it's hard. Can you find the extra support you need through a friend, or perhaps a teacher or counselor?

Sometimes a pregnant woman may not be interested in the things that were important to her only a few weeks ago. If this happens, your family and friends will probably be confused. They may give you advice, too much advice.

When you begin to feel baby move at about 16 weeks, however, you may find you experience a new focus on life.

*Your changing hormones may make you feel moody.*

## You May Have Heartburn

Whatever your age, your last trimester will bring some
different complaints, complaints mostly related to your
body's larger size.

Your uterus is now so big that you can feel pressure in
your stomach area. Heartburn is a common complaint.

**Heartburn? Things you can do:**
- Eat frequent small meals.
- Drink fluids between meals.
- Avoid greasy foods.
- Add more fruits and vegetables to your diet.
- Avoid lying down right after eating. Take a walk
  instead.

*It's not fun being pregnant. You've got all these
responsibilities. And the weight! I gained maybe two
pounds a month for five or six months, then suddenly I
practically blew up. I'm up to 152, and my normal
weight is 120.*

*LaTisha*

LaTisha, at 15, is still growing herself. Gaining up to 40
pounds is okay for pregnant teens whose own bodies are
still developing.

## If Constipation Is a Problem

Many moms have problems with constipation during the
last six weeks or so of pregnancy. The above tactics for
dealing with heartburn will help you avoid this discomfort.

Eating generous amounts of fiber-rich foods such as
fresh fruits and vegetables (raw or lightly cooked with skin
left on when possible), whole-grain cereals, breads, dried
beans and peas, dried fruits (raisins, prunes, apricots, figs)
can help. Drink lots of water in addition to fruit and

vegetable juices and milk.

If constipation is a problem, try a cup of hot water flavored with lemon (no sugar). It might help. If you exercise each day, you're likely to be less bothered with constipation. Walking briskly for half an hour is especially good, along with your prepared childbirth exercises.

## Varicose Veins and Hemorrhoids

Varicose veins and hemorrhoids (varicose veins around the rectum) are clusters of swollen blood vessels. They are more common in women and in certain families, especially those of northern European descent. Pregnancy hormones weaken the blood vessels.

**To prevent varicose veins/hemorrhoids:**
• Avoid standing or sitting for long periods.
• Elevate your feet higher than your hips several times each day.
• Only gain 24-28 pounds in pregnancy (up to 40 pounds if you're under 18).
• Avoid constipation — the extra pushing causes hemorrhoids. So does pushing in labor if it's too soon.
• Don't smoke, and don't wear tight shoes or pants.
• Exercise the muscles of the lower leg (calf muscles) to improve leg circulation. Walking is especially good exercise for you throughout pregnancy.

## If You Can't Sleep

*By eight months, I started getting tired again. Now I'm really tired. I can't get comfortable. I can't sleep.*

LaTisha

Insomnia, or sleeplessness, is a frequent discomfort in the last few months of pregnancy. There are several reasons

*Pillows can help you sleep better.*

and several solutions. Your uterus, now much larger, is pressing against several organs. One result is shortness of breath. Another is back problems.

The illustration above shows you how you can position several pillows under your body to help you feel better. Try it. This is such a relaxing position that you may sleep this way for awhile after delivery, too.

It's better not to sleep on your back toward the end of pregnancy. This helps you avoid squeezing the large blood vessels (the aorta and vena cava) which could reduce the blood supply to both you and baby.

## Dealing with Backaches

*I carried Blair high up all the way up until I had him. I had back pains because I'm short and I was real far out; I was huge. I couldn't stand for a long time, and I had back problems in my fifth month.*

Brooke

The weight you carry now on the front side of your body is pulling against your back. As your spine adapts to this extra weight, you may have backaches.

*Now my back is hurting. I walk a lot but I don't do*
*a lot of exercising like I should. I don't know how to*
*exercise to make my back feel better.*

Marlee, 18 - 6 months pregnant

If you *exercise* throughout your pregnancy, you're less
likely to have pain in your back. Hopefully, you haven't
waited until your last trimester to do so. However, it's
never too late, so join that childbirth preparation class!

**Backache? Things you can do:**

• Heat may make your back feel better. Others find
that ice helps. Most healthcare providers recommend that you don't go in a hot tub (jacuzzi) during
pregnancy. Check with *your* doctor.

• Massage feels good, too, so accept any offers for a
back rub.

• Resting with your legs elevated helps both your
back and your legs.

• Squat down to pick things up from the floor. Avoid
bending forward from your waist.

• Remember to stand with your knees relaxed. This
keeps your back and leg muscles relaxed, too.

• Doing your prenatal exercises regularly can also
help prevent backache.

## Movement from Baby

Healthy babies are very active toward the end of pregnancy. The baby moving around doesn't usually hurt, but
you can feel it.

Between your twenty-eighth and thirtieth week of
pregnancy, your doctor may talk about doing a "kick
count." He may tell you to lie down on your side and

concentrate on how long it takes your baby to move ten times. If it takes longer than two hours, let your doctor know. Kick counts can reassure you that the baby is okay. You may or may not be involved with anyone sexually during your pregnancy. Those who are may have questions about what is okay sexually at this time. Sexual activity is fine with one or two exceptions. Bleeding, pain, or a rupture of the membranes (broken water bag) are reasons to avoid sexual intercourse. Other sexual activities are all right. In fact, many couples experience exceptional closeness during pregnancy.

## Danger Signs

Some events are more than minor discomforts. If any of these happen, ask your health professional what to do:

- Problems with your vision — blurring, double vision, or spots.
- Swelling of your face, fingers, or lower back.
- Headaches — severe, frequent, or continuous.
- Muscular jitteriness or convulsions.
- Severe stomach-ache.
- Persistent vomiting — beyond first trimester, or severe vomiting at any time.
- Fluid discharge from vagina — bleeding or amniotic fluid or increased vaginal discharge.
- Signs of infections — chills, fever, burning on urination, diarrhea.
- Pain in abdomen — severe or unusual.
- Change in fetal movements — absence of fetal movements after quickening (after you have felt fetus moving), any unusual change in pattern or amount.

If you can't reach your healthcare professional, go to the hospital emergency room. Call 911 if you can't get to the emergency room.

## Pregnancy Isn't Permanent

*During pregnancy I had excruciating pain in my tailbone. It could have been the pressure. The last month was horrible because I was so big I could hardly walk. I'd go to the mall, then actually could not walk because I'd get sharp pains. I got sweaty a lot because I'd be so hot. My stomach hit the bread-board in the kitchen because it stuck out so far.*

Courtney, pregnant at 15

Most moms begin to feel permanently pregnant about this time. As we mentioned before, nobody has ever been pregnant forever. That fact doesn't help much, however, when you *feel* that way.

During these last weeks of pregnancy, rest when you can, use make-up, take the time to dress carefully. If you can afford it, buy a new maternity outfit in your favorite color for this "my-pregnancy-is-lasting-forever" time.

Many expectant moms (and dads, too) have dreams about their unborn babies. It's a happy and normal experience. It is not, however, a guarantee as to how your baby will look or what sex s/he will be. Enjoy them for what they are — dreams.

You're likely to have a fairly comfortable pregnancy if you follow the suggestions in this chapter.

*Most important, you can look forward to a new you as your baby's mother.*

*For more information, read **What to Expect When You're Expecting** by Arlene Eisenberg, Heidi E. Murkoff, and Sandee E. Hathaway (Workman Publishing).*

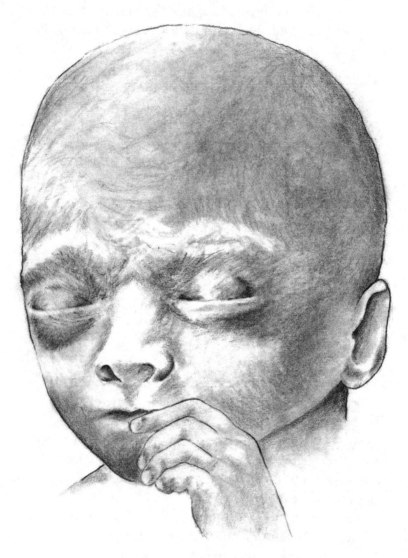

*At 24 weeks your baby is fully formed*
*but not yet ready for life outside.*
*S/he weighs about 1 1/2 pounds.*
*Note: Baby is not drawn to scale. His/her head*
*is much smaller at 24 weeks.*

# 3
# Your Baby's Development

*I remember my first ultrasound when I was almost five months along. He's sitting in there with his thumb in his mouth.*

*Throughout my whole pregnancy from then on, he was kicking me. It was funny, this little tiny thing, and he'd be moving around. I liked that — it made him more real somehow.*

Theo, 19 - Nicklaus, 9 months

*When I first felt Jacob move, I could hardly wait to tell Hal. We talked about how he'd look. That night I dreamed about the baby.*

Sheela, 17 - Jacob, 4 months

## Sperm and Ovum Unite

Each of us has something in common with the baby growing within you. That wonderful thing is that we all began the same way. Our father's sperm united with our mother's ovum and here we are!

Getting here involved a mysterious journey. That first union took place in our mother's fallopian tube. At that point, we looked like a ball of cells. That ball of cells grew rapidly as it moved down the four-inch long tube into the uterus, then spent a day or two deciding just where to implant itself. Your baby was developing like this before you missed your first period. During this time, the number of cells increases rapidly. This process is called *proliferation*.

**Proliferation:** Making a lot of something, usually quickly.

## Female and Male Reproductive Organs

The following diagrams of female and male organs can help you better understand your body and your partner's body. Learning the correct names of these body parts will make it easier to talk with your doctor and your partner.

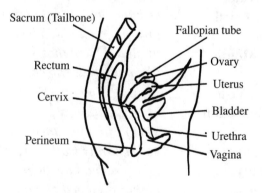

*Female reproductive organs*

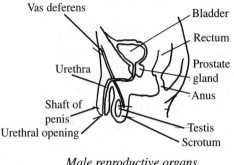

*Male reproductive organs*

---

**Urethra:** Opening where the urine comes out.

**Perineum:** Space between the vagina and rectum.

**Vas deferens:** Tube which delivers sperm during sex.

**Prostate gland:** Makes sperm active.

**Testicles:** Where man's sperm is made.
Semen contains sperm.

**Fallopian Tube:** Part of a woman's body.
The egg moves through it to the utrus.

**Ovum:** The egg a woman's body releases every month.

---

## Cells Continue to Divide

By the time your period is late and you're getting that pregnancy test, the cells within you have begun a process called *differentiation*. Up to now the cells have looked pretty much alike. Now they're beginning to sort themselves out.

---

**Differentiation:** Sorting things out,
putting things together that are alike.

---

Characteristics called "chromosomes" will guide each cell's growth.

---

**Chromosomes:** The basic cell part
containing inherited things.

---

Both mother and father have 23 pairs of these chromosomes. Each parent gives one from each pair to baby. Eye
and hair color are decided this way. The baby's gender is
determined by which chromosome the father gives to baby.

MOM                              DAD

X        X              Y        X

GIRL          BOY
XX            YX

*Dad's chromosome "chooses" boy or girl.*

By the end of your first month of pregnancy,
the embryo is 1/2 inch long. The arms, legs and
shoulders have barely begun to appear. The
eyes are present though we don't think baby
sees yet. Brain cells are already developing.

*Four weeks
drawn to
actual size*

The placenta is also developing. It will provide protein,
estrogen, and progesterone (sex hormones) that are needed
for the development of the baby's brain,
spinal cord, and many other structures.

## Second, Third Months
## (5 - 13½ weeks)

During the next month, your baby
doubles in length and the organs of the
abdomen begin to develop. At eight
weeks the baby is called a fetus. Before

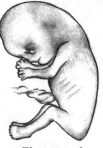

*Eleven weeks
drawn to actual size*

that time, s/he was called an embryo.

There isn't really a skeleton yet as the arms and legs are barely beginning. The body is mainly working on the development of internal organs such as the liver, stomach, gall bladder and spleen. Tiny fingers are beginning to develop. The baby's tongue and teeth can also be found. The heart pumps blood.

During the third month she will grow to about 31/2 to 4 inches in length. Her brain is making very rapid growth at this time. By the end of this month all the parts of her body will be started. The rest of pregnancy will be devoted to fine-tuning them — helping them grow bigger and more efficient and able to operate on their own without your blood supply for nourishment.

During this period your baby's sexual organs develop. Now we could tell whether you're going to have a boy or girl baby.

During this time your breasts may become swollen and tender. The nipples and areola (area around the nipples) will darken.

## Fourth Month Ends (18 weeks)

By the end of the fourth month, baby is six to seven inches long, roughly the size of the flat part of his daddy's hand. The muscles and skin of baby's face now reflect an inherited pattern — you could tell who he looks like!

Tiny fingernails begin to grow. His lungs, the last organ to mature, begin to breathe amniotic fluid.

As your body enlarges, you may

*Sixteen weeks*
*drawn to actual size.*

notice that some days you feel bigger than others. This is partly because the amount of fluid around the baby varies as he breathes and drinks the fluid. You will continue to notice this variation throughout pregnancy.

Incidentally, when your healthcare provider talks about how far along in your pregnancy you are, she usually refers to the number of weeks or months LMP. This means the amount of time since your last menstrual period. When you talk about the number of months you're pregnant, you're probably talking about the time since you conceived. If your timing doesn't match your doctor's, this might be the reason. Estimated date of confinement (EDC) means due date.

## Prenatal Visits Lead to Healthy Babies

Your healthcare provider may discuss a procedure called an *ultrasound*. This is done in a healthcare facility.

---

**Ultrasound:** An examination using sonar or radio-like waves to trace the outline of the baby in the uterus.

---

An ultrasound, which doesn't hurt at all, is done mainly to see how far the baby's growth has progressed and to confirm the due date. It can also determine the presence of certain birth defects and sometimes the gender of the baby. If you have an ultrasound, you may receive a copy of the picture of the baby — although it won't look like a photograph.

Frequent and important blood tests will be done during your prenatal health care visits. One will show your blood type. Another is called AFP (alpha feta protein), and it measures the protein in your blood. It also gives clues about how your baby is developing.

Another test sometimes done at about 16 weeks gestation is called *amniocentesis.* In this test, fluid from the uterus is removed with a long needle and sent to a special laboratory. This fluid can be tested to reveal the baby's gender, and many other characteristics including such rare genetic conditions as Down Syndrome. This test doesn't hurt much. It's like any injection with a needle.

About 75 percent of pregnant women are given an ultrasound, but only five to ten percent take the amniocentesis test. If you have an amniocentesis, you won't know the results for about two weeks, and they're reported like a blood test. If this is done, you can get a picture of your baby's chromosomes.

*All prenatal visits are very important, including those short ones in the middle of your pregnancy.*

## You'll Feel Him Move

By the twentieth week, halfway through pregnancy, your baby will weigh about 20 ounces and be about 12 inches long. Since the baby opens and closes her eyes, we know she is experiencing a variety of things. She senses light and dark. She may suck her thumb at times. Now you can feel her moving around inside of you. This movement of the baby is sometimes called *quickening.*

The doctor can easily hear your baby's heart beating now, and will check that every time you go in for a visit. Baby's ears are also developed by this time, and she sometimes moves in response to loud sounds.

A few years ago, researchers tried to learn what baby hears at this stage. One woman they interviewed was a cello player. During her pregnancy she was preparing for a musical performance. She played a favorite song every day during her pregnancy. The cello rested against her body where the baby was most likely to hear it. She discovered

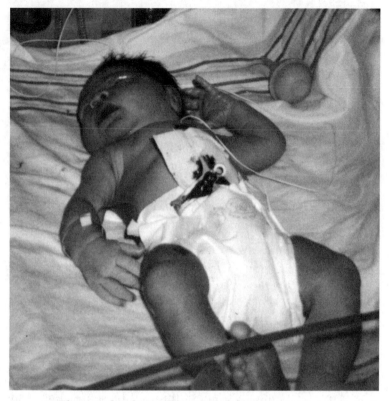

*The result of nine months of development . . .*

that after her baby was born, she could calm him by playing
that same song.

## Sixth Month — Not Ready to Be Born

By the 24th week your baby should weigh about 1 1/2
pounds. She now has hair, eyelashes, and that fine baby
hair you may have noticed on newborn babies. It is called
*lanugo*. The baby also is covered with a creamy substance
called *vernix*. This is a cream that nature provides to make
her skin soft. When your baby is born you may notice it,
especially in the folds of her skin.

Baby can now cry, but very weakly. If born at this time,

his lungs probably wouldn't be ready to work well, but some babies born this early do survive. Many, however, have life-long disabilities.

About this time, as mentioned on page 43, the doctor will talk about "kick counts," the number of times baby kicks per hour. Count baby's kicks while you're lying down after dinner. If baby is growing well, she will become very active during the last few months of pregnancy.

## Baby Gets Fatter

During the last ten weeks of pregnancy, the baby gains weight by making fat. She has had very little fat up to now. Most of us don't especially like the idea of adding fat, but it is an important part of the body. It is a reserve of energy for rapid growth which will continue even after the baby is born. It also insulates your baby from heat and cold.

Fat gives the body softness and curves which cushion impact and make the pleasant cuddly feeling we associate with babies. While theoretically your baby can live outside the uterus at this time, most babies who are born before 36 weeks gestation spend several weeks in the hospital "finishing" their development. They often suffer complications of their immaturity which may or may not be outgrown.

At 40 weeks, the average baby weighs 71/2 pounds and is 20-22 inches long. His mother will have gained at least 25 pounds during her pregnancy. The rest of the weight she gained is for her body's use.

Your baby's journey from conception to delivery is a wonderful and fascinating journey. The next two chapters tell you how you can help make that journey a healthy one for your child. *It's up to you.*

*Your baby eats what you eat.*

# 4

# Eating Right for Baby and You

*I ate good because I wanted a healthy baby. I loved him already, and I knew if I ate bad, he could be all little, and that scared me a lot.*

Carole, 15 - Kevin, 3 months

*My boyfriend eats vegetables, and I find myself craving vegetables. I drink a lot of milk. I don't really like it, but I drink it because I know the baby needs it. I take my vitamins all the time, and even though I don't like meat too much, I make sure I have enough protein. I want the healthiest baby possible.*

Anessa, pregnant at 17

## Your Baby Eats What You Eat

"If she doesn't start eating better, I'm getting out of here before I'm supposed to," says the fetus in "Inside My Mom," a video produced several years ago by March of Dimes Birth Defects Foundation. The hero of the film was a cartoon fetus who was concerned about his mother's diet. His point was that babies of poorly nourished mothers are likely to be born too early.

The little fetus continued to talk about his mother's eating habits. "Oh good! She's finally getting me something to eat," he exclaimed.

In the next scene, his mother was buying from a junk food machine. The little fetus moaned, "Oh no! Just a candy bar. Doesn't she know I need *real* food?"

Before long, however, his mother's doctor convinced her that she should eat healthy foods so she would have a healthy baby. She started eating the foods she and her baby needed, and the little fetus was delighted.

Remember, if you're under 18 and pregnant, you need all the good foods an older pregnant woman needs *plus* an extra glass of milk. You need that extra milk because your bones are still growing.

You also need to drink 6-8 glasses of water each day. Water is much better than soda for you and for your baby.

*You need to take care of yourself and eat right. My sister's baby was barely five pounds when he was born. I think it was because she didn't eat right. All she'd do was drink soda and eat chips and candy.*

Alice Ann, 15 - Vincent, 3 weeks

You know now how your baby is developing inside you. Your next step is to learn what you can do to help your baby grow. Is your goal to make a good baby without gaining too much weight?

Good nutrition throughout pregnancy is essential if both mother and baby are to develop well.

> *I changed my eating. When I got pregnant I started eating more and taking my prenatal vitamins. I don't eat junk food.*
>
> Emmy, 18 - Zalena, 4 months

Okay, so what do you need to eat when you're pregnant? There is no magic formula other than what you've already heard about nutrition in your health classes. Only now it's your baby who will suffer if you eat only junk food.

Every day you need food from the following food groups:

* **Milk, yogurt, and cheese group — 4 servings**
* **Vegetable Group — 3-5 servings**
* **Fruit Group — 2-4 servings**
* **Bread, cereal, rice, and pasta group — 6 servings**
* **Meat, poultry, fish, eggs, dry beans, and nuts group — 3 servings**
* **Fats and sweets — Use in moderation.**

You needed these foods before you were pregnant, but now you need even more of some of them. If you're nauseated, have heartburn, or changes in your appetite, eating will be a special problem for you.

Do you ever have heartburn? Fats, spicy foods, coffee, chocolate, spearmint and peppermint all may contribute to heartburn. So do alcohol and nicotine. If you don't eat these foods, drink, or smoke, and still have heartburn, try smaller meals. Eat more often, and drink liquids between meals.

A midnight snack may help prevent morning sickness. It

also may help solve sleeping problems at the end of pregnancy.

Your family may like to eat fast-foods often, or they may have other eating habits that don't fit into the best pregnancy diet. If so, you need to consider your reality, what's possible and available for you to eat. You work from there to make the healthiest choices possible from the foods available. It's important to you *and* your baby.

## Good Nutrition Helps Prevent Eclampsia

Another important issue in pregnancy is eclampsia (pregnancy induced hypertension or toxemia). Eclampsia is a condition some mothers develop during the last few weeks of pregnancy.

---

**Signs and Symptoms of Eclampsia**

- **Extremely high blood pressure** (That's why they always take your blood pressure at the doctor's.)
- **Severe and persistent headaches**
- **Blurry vision**
- **Sudden, rapid weight gain with severe swelling in the legs, face, fingers, or lower back**
- **Eventually, convulsions or jittery muscles**

---

Some swelling is normal because your body is storing liquid for its future needs. However, a sudden, rapid weight gain with severe swelling in your legs, ankles, and fingers could be a symptom of eclampsia.

Some people feel eating too much salt causes this swelling. If your healthcare provider notices any symptoms of eclampsia, she may ask you to cut out most of the salt in your diet. If this happens, you need to cooperate. Generally, however, if you're eating a well balanced diet, you can eat a reasonable amount of salt without worrying. If you have questions about this issue, ask your healthcare provider.

Eclampsia can be a serious problem. It's the main cause of childbirth-related deaths of mothers in the developed nations of the world.

We're not trying to frighten you. We're also not suggesting that if you eat poorly once in a while you're going to die. The message, however, is that we're not talking simply about a beauty issue as we discuss nutrition in pregnancy.

Two things are known to help prevent eclampsia. One is regular prenatal care. *See your healthcare provider regularly.* The other is eating enough protein including dairy products.

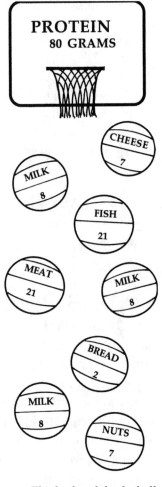

*Think of each basketball as a serving of protein. Put them all together and you have a day's supply of protein.*

## Importance of Protein

Babies whose mothers eat plenty of protein have more brain cells than do babies whose mothers eat less than three servings of protein foods each day during pregnancy. More brain cells mean a smarter baby!

Protein foods include all kinds of meat, fish, and poultry. (However, because of risk of mercury poisoning, the Food and Drug Administration advises pregnant women not to eat shark, tilefish, king mackerel and swordfish.)

Peanut butter, refried beans with cheese, baked beans, and eggs are also high in protein. So is the milk you drink. Cereal, bread, pasta, and a few other foods also contain some protein. You need at least 60 grams of protein. If you're still growing (under 18), you're wise to eat about 80 grams a day. Labels on packages tell you the amount of protein in a serving of the food.

*I changed what I ate. Before, I didn't eat a lot. Like at school I'd eat Cheetos and not much else. When I was pregnant, I ate a lot. I didn't eat junk food. I couldn't eat it at all — I'd throw up. I ate chicken, fish, shrimps, vegetables. I drank a lot of milk.*

Ynez, 16 - Lenny, 4 months

*Before Ynez was pregnant she wouldn't even taste fish. Then after she got pregnant we ate a lot of seafood.*

Del, 20 - Lenny's father

## Milk for Baby's Bones, Teeth

It's hard to think of a pregnant mom's diet without thinking about milk. Besides being a good source of the much needed protein, milk provides calcium. Your growing baby needs a lot of calcium for building bones and teeth.

If you like milk, drink four or five glasses each day. If you don't drink milk, get your calcium from other foods. See the cow drawing for some foods which supply the same amount of protein and calcium as one large glass of milk.

It's okay to add chocolate to your milk — but remember you're adding calories, too. Some people worry about the caffeine in chocolate, but a glass of chocolate milk does not contain enough caffeine to hurt your baby. One way to reduce calories is to use low- (1 percent) or non-fat milk.

**BABY NEEDS**

4 servings of milk
OR
trade <u>one</u> glass for <u>one</u> of these:
1 slice American Cheese
6 oz. yogurt
1" cube any cheese
1/2 cup ice cream
1/2 cup cottage cheese

*The cow suggests possible substitutes for milk.*

Adding fruit to six ounces of plain yogurt gives you even more protein than six ounces of premixed yogurt. You can add fruit, fresh or canned, as you eat it. Mixing the fruit in yourself also saves you money. Do other family members tend to eat your yogurt? Perhaps they'll be more likely to leave the plain yogurt for you and your baby.

Melting a slice of cheese on a piece of bread for breakfast or lunch adds the protein of bread to your meal along with the calcium and protein in the cheese.

## Fruits and Vegetables

Fruits and vegetables contain water and carbohydrates which give you lots of energy. Most important, they are good sources of vitamins and minerals. Generally, the darker the color, the richer the food is in vitamins and minerals. For instance, broccoli and spinach are richer in vitamins than plain lettuce or celery.

Eating a variety of fruits and vegetables gives a good

*You have lots of choices for your fruits and vegetables.*

balance in your diet. Fruits and vegetables are as good for you raw as they are cooked. If you eat tomato and lettuce with your hamburger, you get a serving of vegetables.

If you don't like vegetables, you can get most of these nutrients in fruit. Fruit on your cereal counts as one of the four servings you need daily.

Eating plenty of fruits and vegetables also helps prevent constipation.

## Cereals and Bread

*In my fifth month the doctor said I was very ane-mic. He told me to take two iron pills a day, and they made me constipated. So I'd eat a lot of fruit and drink a lot of liquids, and that helped. I ate a lot of fiber, too.*

Chelsea, 19 - Clancy, 2 months

Almost everyone likes the foods in this group. They include all the cereals and all the breads as well as spa-ghetti, macaroni, rice, corn, oats, tortillas, and pizza crust. Choose sugar-free cereals because of the lower calorie and higher fiber content. The fiber helps prevent constipation, a common complaint during pregnancy.

Another plus for this group is that they contain some protein. If you eat the six servings you need daily, you'll have as much protein as you'd get in half a serving of meat or fish.

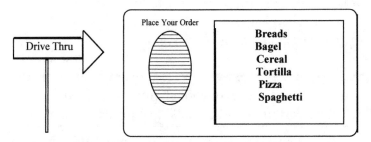

*You can get your breads and cereals while you're out.*

## Take Your Vitamins

*I've always had problems eating — food isn't appealing to me. They put me on bed rest and had me drink all these double milk shakes.*

*I went into preterm labor, and Delila was born three weeks early. She weighed 5 pounds, 13 ounces.*

Elisa Marie, 15 - Delila, 9 months

Few of us eat a perfect diet every day. For that reason, and because you and your baby need lots of vitamins and minerals, your doctor will recommend that you take prenatal vitamins.

Sometimes moms complain that the vitamins leave an aftertaste. If that's a problem for you, try taking your vitamin after a larger meal, whether that's lunch or dinner. You'll digest your vitamin more slowly with your meal which may cut out the aftertaste.

You may already have regular vitamins at home, or you

may see a brand that's cheaper than those prescribed by
your doctor. Is it okay to take those instead? Not really.
Prenatal vitamins contain extra amounts of vitamins and
minerals you especially need during pregnancy. Most
important are folic acid and iron.

> *I was really sick. I was anemic, and they were*
> *always taking blood from me. The first few months I*
> *didn't want to eat at all. I always gagged and threw*
> *up my first month to my fifth month.*

Elisa Marie

---

**Anemia:** A lack of enough iron in the blood
which causes tiredness, a "dull" feeling, and weakness.

---

Pregnant women need more iron because they're making
additional blood for themselves and their baby. Recent
research also showed that pregnant teens who take enough
iron every day have a far better attention span than
pregnant students who are careless about getting enough.

*More milk for baby and you.*

So, stick to those prenatal vitamins all during your pregnancy. In fact, some doctors recommend that moms continue taking them for a few weeks after delivery because the vitamins help them feel better.

If there's another child around, be sure to keep your prenatal vitamins out of reach. The high iron levels in prenatal vitamins can make a young child quite sick.

## Limit the Fat

*This time I'm not going to overeat. I'm going to watch my weight, eat good, but not gain too much. Last time I went from 115 to 180 pounds. I'm still ten pounds away from my normal weight — and I'm pregnant again!*

Eileen, 18 - Jackie, 17 months

What about fat and calories? How a food is prepared is as important as what it contains before it's cooked. For instance, you add about 90 calories when you fry eggs in a tablespoon of butter. Fried eggs are fine if they're prepared in a teflon-coated pan without added fat. Adding a teaspoon or so of water will keep them from sticking, yet won't change the taste at all.

Other foods high in fat include lunch meat, hot dogs, sweet breads, desserts such as pie or cream puffs, and, of course, anything deep fried.

## Calories Count

*When I got pregnant, it was exciting. I think I ate everything in sight. I did a lot of walking, but I gained a lot of weight anyhow. That's why I'm so heavy now.*

LuAnn, 20 - Eddie, 4

When you're low on energy, it's tempting to have a candy bar or doughnut. Within an hour, however, that

energy surge is gone and you're feeling listless again.
Snacks such as fresh fruit, peanuts, yogurt, or milk will
give you energy that lasts longer. As a bonus, these foods
give baby more energy, too.

Calories do count during pregnancy. A pregnant teenager should be able to eat 2500 to 3000 calories per day. If
you stay within this limit and you're getting a reasonable
amount of exercise, you'll probably gain between 24 and
28 pounds, the amount recommended by most doctors.

Ideally, you'll gain 2-4 pounds during your first three
months of pregnancy, plus three or four pounds *each* month
during your remaining six months. Your weight gain will
include 6-8 pounds of baby. The rest of your added weight
is caused by your larger breasts, bigger uterus, amniotic

*Choose an apple instead of French fries.*

fluid, and the placenta. In addition, your body will have a higher fluid volume during pregnancy.

If you're 17 or younger and still growing, you may need to gain more weight, up to 40 pounds. It's important that you show a slow steady gain from about your eighth week until your baby is born.

So often pregnant teenagers think that if they gain much weight, they'll not be able to get back into their jeans and bikinis. If they were eating a lot of of junk food before pregnancy (as many non-pregnant teenagers seem to do), they may continue this way of eating.

If she has French fries and a coke for a snack very often, a pregnant 16-year-old either won't have any appetite for the nutritious foods she needs, or her weight will shoot up far higher than she or her healthcare provider wants. Gaining 50 to 60 pounds during those nine months isn't healthy either.

## The Fast-Food Dilemma

Many people eat fast-foods. Some teens appear almost to live on hamburgers, French fries, and soda. Sometimes people say fast-foods are junk foods. Some of them, such as sodas, add empty calories to your diet. If you know what's good for you, however, you can continue to enjoy occasional fast-foods without feeling guilty.

Let's compare some choices:

|  | PROTEIN | CALORIES | FAT |
|---|---|---|---|
| Double bacon cheeseburger | 42 gm | 890 | 55% |
| Reg. size fries | 4 gm | 420 | 45% |
| Reg. size soda | 0 | 243 | 0 |
| **Total** | **46 gm** | **1553** | **44%** |

Perhaps this doesn't look so bad. You get half the calories and half the protein you need each day. This meal,
however, has some glaring faults:

• It doesn't leave much room for calories for the rest
  of your day.

• It includes very little vegetable and no fruit.

• It's high in fat which means more fat on *your* body.
Ideally, your meals will contain no more than 30 percent
fat. *Above all, avoid super-sizing, even though it's
tempting!*

Now let's compare the hamburger, fries, and soda with
chicken, salad, and milk:

|  | PROTEIN | CALORIES | FAT |
|---|---|---|---|
| Charbroiled BBQ chicken ( not fried) sandwich | 25 gm | 310 | 17% |
| 10 oz. low fat milk | 13 gm | 175 | 2% |
| Salad with 2 oz. bleu cheese dressing | 6 gm | 300 | 75% |
| **Total** | **44 gm** | **785** | **36%** |

This gives you almost as much protein (plenty for one
meal) as the hamburger, French fries, and soda. If you eat
chicken, milk, and salad, you'll get only about one quarter
of your daily calorie allowance. Even with the salad dress-
ing, it has less fat.

You'll feel full, you'll feel good — and you won't need
extra walking to get rid of calories.

Be careful of foods described as "lite." For instance, one
fast-food chain's "lite" potato is more than 50 percent fat,
contains almost 300 calories, and has only seven grams of
protein. That's *not* a good deal nutritionwise.

## Eating for Your Baby

To plan meals, choose foods from each of the food groups listed on page 61. Every day plan to have three protein group servings, four dairy foods, six breads and cereals, two to four fruits, and three to five vegetables.

Stay away from foods that have lots of fat or are "empty" calories. If you eat like this, you should feel good and have a healthy baby.

Eat the foods you need all through your pregnancy. *Your baby will appreciate you!*

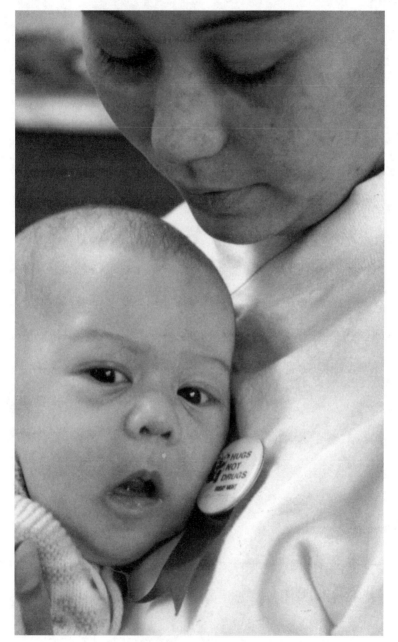

*Her pin says it — "Hugs, not drugs for baby."*

# 5

# "No" to Smoking, Drugs, Alcohol

- **Smoking Harms Fetus**
- **Baby Can't "Breathe"**
- **Smokers May Have Smaller Babies**
- **Fetal Alcohol Syndrome (FAS)**
- **Drugs and Pregnancy**
- **"No" to Over-the-Counter Drugs**

*I was into pot and alcohol pretty bad. Once after I was a few weeks pregnant, I got mad at Jim, so I got drunk, and I was scared. But Orlando's okay, and now I'm going to stay clear of it all. I don't want to be afraid next time. I know that drinking or smoking dope is not going to help matters. It'll make it worse.*

Holly, 17 - Orlando, 5 months

*I wanted to quit smoking when I got pregnant, but I couldn't. I knew all the health risks to myself and to my baby, but that wasn't helping. Finally I took a stop-smoking class at school, mostly because I needed the credit to graduate.*

*You had to write down every time you wanted a cigarette, what you were doing at the time, and what you could do instead of smoking. I decided to see if it would work. I was already several months pregnant, but I managed to quit.*

Angelica, 20 - Shaun, 3

Some people, when they're confused or concerned about something, turn to drugs, alcohol or smoking to comfort themselves. When we consider the danger to the fetus if the mother smokes (including pot), uses drugs, or drinks liquor, however, it's clear that these activities are a form of abusing a child — even though that child is not yet born.

## Smoking Harms Fetus

Do you smoke? If you're pregnant, you could do you and your child a big favor by stopping.

*I used to smoke a lot. Then one day Tim told me he didn't want to kiss me because I smelled like an ashtray. Then Angel, who was 2, was breaking up my cigarettes and leaving them all over. Tim said, "See, Angel wants you to quit."*

*I said, "Everyone in my family smokes."*

*He said, "Well, you don't have to."*

*He wouldn't buy me cigarettes. He said he'd buy me anything else. Finally when I got pregnant with Kenny, Tim and I sat down and I told him, "I think it's going to be real hard for me. My body is telling me I want to smoke and the baby is telling me I shouldn't smoke." I did have one terrible week. I went a whole week without smoking, and I ate and I ate and I ate.*

*Then after that one week, I didn't want to smoke. In fact, smoke bothered me. My family would blow*

*smoke in my face because they thought I'd want a
cigarette. I'd tell them I didn't want to smoke.
And then I realized how a smoker smells. I can't
stand it. My brother smokes, and when he walks in, he
smells awful. I'm glad I quit.*

Meghan, 25 - Angel, 8; Kenny, 6; Jose, 2; Leon, 8 months

## Baby Can't "Breathe"

*I went to the doctor when I was four months preg-
nant. When I finally accepted the fact I was pregnant,
I cut back on my smoking. Then in my last month I got
this real hang-up about smoking — even though I
hadn't seen Karl yet. I suddenly wanted to do this for
him (or her — I didn't know which yet). So I just quit.
Then I couldn't stand someone else smoking — it
almost made me sick.*

*I'm still not smoking. I feel I should do everything I
can to influence Karl not to smoke. If I get upset and
want to smoke, I get a coke or a glass of water or
sometimes a carrot or a toothpick, anything but a
cigarette. I know if I smoke even one, I'll start again,
so I simply can't have that first one.*

Kimberly, 17 - Karl, 23 months

Each time you smoke, your baby has a hard time
"breathing" inside you. A fetus doesn't breathe as we do, of
course, but when his mother smokes, he gets less oxygen.

Recent research shows that the fetus may be in distress
when his mother is in a smoke-filled room. Being in a room
with smokers causes the baby to be more uneasy since he
isn't getting enough oxygen.

## Smokers May Have Smaller Babies

*As soon as I found out I was pregnant, I quit
smoking because they say you can have a premature*

*baby. I didn't want to take any chances. It's only nine*
*months not to smoke, and you might as well not risk it.*
*After all, it's another life inside you.*

Cheryl, 15 - Racquelle, 2 months

Pregnant women who smoke cigarettes tend to have
smaller babies who gain weight slowly. That's because the
baby doesn't get enough oxygen. Being born too small is
the major cause of infant illness and infant death. There are
more miscarriages, stillbirths, and sudden infant deaths
(SIDS) among babies whose mothers smoked. These babies
also have more colds and pneumonia than other babies.

Once we researched the effects of smoking among
students in our school. Thirty-nine babies were born to
students in our special program for pregnant teenagers that
year. Four of the babies weighed less than six pounds. The
mothers of three of those babies smoked during pregnancy.
Almost no one else in the class smoked.

Incidentally, Cheryl's comment above, "After all, it's
only nine months not to smoke" doesn't make sense if she
wants her baby to be as healthy as possible. Children whose
parents smoke get nearly twice as many colds, sore throats,
and ear infections as children whose parents don't smoke.

## Fetal Alcohol Syndrome (FAS)

*Friends would say, "Oh, just a little (liquor) won't*
*hurt." But I didn't. I was always trying to think back*
*to those first two or three months, wondering if I had*
*done things that would harm her. I worried that my*
*baby might not be all right. Smoking is bad enough,*
*but drugs and alcohol — I don't see how anybody*
*could do that during pregnancy.*

Beth, 18 - Patty, 3 weeks

If you're pregnant, think before you drink — then don't!

Fetal Alcohol Syndrome (FAS) is a condition affecting babies whose mothers drank alcohol during pregnancy. We know that alcohol can cause a pattern of physical and mental defects in the fetus such as mental retardation.

An FAS baby may be abnormally small at birth, especially in head size. Unlike most small newborns, the FAS baby never catches up in growth. Most of these youngsters have smaller than average brains resulting in mild to severe mental retardation. They are often jittery and have behavior problems. Almost half of the FAS babies have heart defects which may require surgery. Even small amounts of alcohol can cause facial abnormalities.

> *"Fetal Alcohol Syndrome (FAS)*
> *is one birth defect*
> *the mother alone can prevent."*

The worst thing for a pregnant woman to do is go on a binge. Lots of drinking at once is especially risky for the fetus. There is no known safe level of alcohol use for pregnant women, particularly during the first three months when the baby's vital organs are developing.

"To be safe, forget about drinking throughout pregnancy," cautions Anita Gallegos, former Director of Community Services, March of Dimes Birth Defects Foundation, Southern California Chapter. "This is one birth defect the mother alone can prevent."

## Drugs and Pregnancy

*The day I found out I was pregnant, no more drugs for me. My mom did drugs when she was pregnant with me and my sisters, and we all have something wrong with us. I can't do that to my kid. And before, my sister-in-law did drugs, and her baby passed away*

*when he was a month old. I cared a lot about my*
*baby. No more drugs for me.*

Bridget, 18 - Caelin, 2 1/2; Barnaby, 6 months

Taking drugs during pregnancy is endangering your
child. Don't take any unless your doctor prescribes them.
Illegal drugs have lifelong effects on babies. A baby exposed to drugs before she is born may be mentally retarded
and have learning disabilities, language delays, hyperactiv-
ity, poor play skills, and other conditions that interfere with
normal life. Babies who are born addicted also often have
permanent physical disabilities. If they are identified at
birth as addicted, they may not be permitted to be with their
mother. Instead, they could be placed in foster care.

Learning disabilities may not show up until the child
goes to school. Many of the effects of cocaine, crack, and
crystal (crank) are not noticed at birth, and the parents may

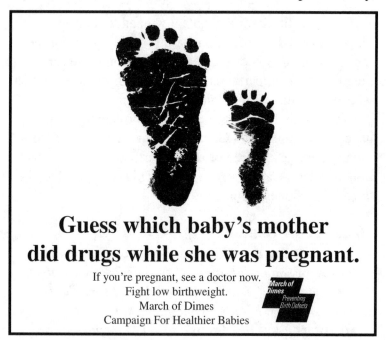

**Guess which baby's mother
did drugs while she was pregnant.**

If you're pregnant, see a doctor now.
Fight low birthweight.
March of Dimes
Campaign For Healthier Babies

March of Dimes
Preventing
Birth Defects

think they were lucky. Crack, cocaine, and crystal all have the same effects. All three cause small holes in the brain.

Children prenatally exposed to drugs are likely to have social problems that keep them from making friends easily. How lonely they must be.

Marijuana smoking also affects your unborn baby. Besides reducing the baby's oxygen supply, the results of the drug can cause a baby to have a stroke and/or permanent brain damage.

Babies born to mothers who are addicted to heroin are likely to be pathetic little creatures who go through withdrawal after birth. These tiny babies experience the same kind of agony an adult experiences who, after becoming addicted to heroin, goes off it cold turkey.

## "No" to Over-the-Counter Drugs

Most of us know not to take "hard" drugs during pregnancy. But did you know that drugs sold "over-the-counter" can also be a problem to a fetus? The right dose for mother generally means baby gets a huge overdose.

Many drugs have been shown to be harmful to the fetus, so many that March of Dimes literature stresses, "Take no drugs, not even a nose spray, aspirin, or Tums, unless your doctor prescribes it." And your doctor will undoubtedly agree with the March of Dimes. Laxatives are especially dangerous during pregnancy.

There is no good time to use drugs, alcohol, or nicotine, but during pregnancy is the worst time. Help your baby to a healthy start.

*Don't drink, smoke, or do drugs!*

> For more information, see **Infants and Children with Prenatal Alcohol and Drug Exposure** by Keeta DeStefano Lewis (Sunrise River Press).

# PREGNANT?
# Adoption
# Is an
# Option

*BY*
## Jeanne
## Warren
## Lindsay

*Teen birthparents tell their stories.*

# 6

# For Some —
# Adoption Is an Option

*I was 14 when I got pregnant. I wasn't expecting it — we used birth control, but the condom broke.*

*I didn't tell my parents. My dad knew, and Mom found out from her friend. She was mad at me — she wanted me to get an abortion.*

*My boyfriend and I weren't ever really together. He told me he didn't want anything to do with the baby. We talked while I was pregnant, but we weren't together. He said he'd pay for an abortion, but I didn't want that.*

*I told him I was considering adoption. He never decided anything. He just went along with it.*

Carmen - placed her baby for adoption

You may be thinking, "Me? Make an adoption plan?
You're crazy!" In any group of pregnant teens, a few may
consider the adoption option. Even fewer will actually
carry out the adoption plan. Nevertheless, we're spending a
chapter on this subject for several reasons:

- If you're one of the few who considers adoption, you
  need information, encouragement, and support.
- If someone you know considers an adoption plan for
  her child, she needs your support.
- You or someone you know may be adopted. You (and
  everyone else) should know that birthparents don't
  want to "give their baby away." It takes a great deal
  of love and courage to place one's child with another
  family through adoption.
- You may know adoptive parents, or you may adopt a
  child some day. You need to know the extremely
  important role the birthparents play in adoption.

It's also important that you know you still have choices.
Ideally, young women and their partners, pregnant before
they expected to be, will develop a parenting plan *and* an
adoption plan.

If they decide to parent their child themselves, they are
likely to feel more positive, knowing they considered
another choice, and parenting is their decision. They were
not trapped into early parenting because there was no other
choice. Knowing one has choices is freeing.

## Adoption Is Changing

*I got pregnant three months before I graduated. I
didn't know anything about adoption — it's not talked
about much. But I was lucky to be working with a girl
who had gone through an open adoption, and I knew
about it because she was very open.*

*If it hadn't been for her, I might never have thought about adoption.*

Maggie, 17 - placed her baby for adoption

Some people think placing one's baby for adoption means the birthmother will never see him again. For a good many years, this was true in agency adoptions and in most independent adoptions. However, the practice of adoption in the United States has changed a great deal. "Open" adoption is now possible in most areas.

Today birthparents can generally choose the adoptive family for their baby. No longer do they have to "give the baby away" and never see their child again if they make an adoption plan. For some, this kind of open adoption makes an adoption decision more possible.

*The open adoption made the entire difference. If I never saw her again it would be harder. I get letters, cards, pictures. The old adoption — I could never have done that and not know where she is.*

*I would be raising her now which wouldn't have been a bad thing. I love her very much, but I feel they can give her so much more than I can, and they're more ready.*

*I feel you have to be emotionally ready to raise a child, and I don't think I am. I've seen a lot of teenage girls out there struggling to raise their babies. And I've seen the kid's situation going back and forth between Mommy and Daddy and the parents constantly fighting.*

The birthparents' adoption counselor may show them several descriptions of possible adoptive couples, and they choose the one they think would make the best parents. Some adoption centers encourage the pregnant woman (and her partner if possible) to interview several couples in person before deciding who should parent the baby.

This may happen several weeks or even months before the child is born, and the birthmother may spend time with the chosen adoptive parents during her pregnancy. Sometimes she invites them to be in the delivery room when the baby is born. The birthparents and the adoptive parents may plan to continue to see each other occasionally after the baby's adoption is finalized.

Some adoptive parents, sadly, have not kept their promise to continue a relationship with their baby's birthparent(s). Several states, however, including California and Washington, now provide legal support for open adoption agreements.

"Get educated as to what open adoption means," suggests Brenda Romanchik, Director, Insight, a non-profit organization that educates on open adoption. "When you talk with an agency counselor, ask exactly what they mean by open adoption."

If you have questions or would like to know of an agency or adoption cener in your area that helps facilitate truly open adoptions, contact Brenda, 877.879.0669 or 248.543.0997. Or see her web site, openadoptioninsight.org>

From a legal standpoint, the adoption decision cannot be made until after the baby is born. The birthmother is under absolutely no obligation to carry out her adoption plan. If, after she sees her baby, she decides to parent, she has as much right as any other mother to do so.

If you or another pregnant teen is interested in learning more about adoption, you/she should contact an adoption counselor. You might go to a licensed adoption agency or to an independent adoption center.

A good counselor, of course, will not try to talk you into

placing your child with another family. The counselor's role is to help you look at your options so *you* can make the best decision possible for you and for your baby.

## Counseling Is Important

It's important that both the potential adoptive parents and the birthparents receive counseling. Adoption is a crisis for everyone involved. Discussing the various issues with someone not directly involved often helps one deal with those issues.

There should be no charge to the birthparent(s) for counseling. This is usually included in the fee the adoptive parents pay when they adopt a child. Their fee also covers the legal costs, and may include prenatal and delivery expenses for the birthmother.

In many states, it is also legal for the adoptive parents to pay "necessary living expenses" for the birthmother during at least the latter part of her pregnancy. It is not legal for the adoptive parents to pay the birthparents a direct fee in exchange for their baby. Babies are not for sale.

---

*Good counseling is extremely important
for all those involved in adoption planning.*

---

Licensed agencies usually provide good counseling services for both the birthparents and the adoptive parents. Independent adoption may simply mean birthparents choose an adoptive family. Then the adoptive family hires a lawyer to handle the legal work.

Many times in independent adoption no one receives much, if any, counseling. More and more, however, independent adoption centers are being set up to provide not only legal assistance in adoption, but also the all-important counseling for birth and adoptive parents.

To repeat, good counseling is extremely important for all those involved in adoption planning.

## Father's Rights in Adoption

*The father signed the papers but he didn't get involved at all. He wasn't there when Jenae was born. Later he asked me if he could have a picture of his daughter.*

*I gave it to him because I know he missed out on something wonderful. He has a picture, but no memories of Jenae.*

Kerry Ann, 17 - placed her baby for adoption

Adoption laws vary a great deal from state to state and from province to province. Generally the father, as well as the mother, must sign the adoption papers. In some states, the man named as the father may sign one of three legal documents:

---

### Father's Legal Options

1. He can give his permission for the adoption to proceed.
2. He can deny that he is the father of the child.
3. He can formally give up all his rights to the child.

---

State laws vary as to what will be done if the named father refuses to sign anything. If he is assumed to be the father, and he won't sign adoption papers, the adoption may be delayed or denied.

Counseling for birthfathers is important, too. If the birthmother is able to select the adoptive parents, it's a good idea for her or her counselor to encourage the father to be involved in the process.

If he has a chance to discuss his feelings, he may realize the adoption plan is a loving and caring choice, possibly the best choice for him and the birthmother as well as for their child.

## Adoption Planning Is Difficult

*Teens tend to think, "My baby will love me. I'll dress him up all cute and everybody will love me, too." But they aren't looking at the late nights, the crying. They aren't thinking, "How am I going to get to the doctor when I can't even drive yet?" I didn't like relying on other people.*

Nita, 15, placed her 3-month-old baby for adoption

Even considering an adoption plan takes courage. Many women bond with their baby during pregnancy. When the baby starts moving, s/he may suddenly become "real."

Making an adoption plan means looking into the future and carefully attempting to judge one's resources and capabilities for parenting. These are some of the questions a pregnant teen might ask herself as she considers her baby's future:

- Am I ready to be a parent 24 hours a day?

- Am I willing to be responsible for my child? Or am I relying on my parents for assistance? If so, have they agreed to provide the help I'm expecting?

- Do I have a realistic plan for supporting this child financially?

The questions could go on and on. The point is to look at one's choices, think of the good things and the bad things about each choice, and then make a decision, the best decision possible for you and your baby.

## Grandparents' Feelings

*I was five months pregnant when his mom came
over and begged me to give the baby up for adoption.
I was crying and crying, and she wouldn't listen to a
word I was saying.*

*She said I was so immature, that I was just a little
girl and didn't know what I was doing. My mom was
real mad.*

Kristin, pregnant at 15

Your parents may have firm opinions about adoption.
They may be absolutely opposed to adoption. Perhaps they
say, "No child of ours will be given away." Or they may
push adoption. It's hard for some parents to realize that the
*birthparents* make the decision for or against adoption.

Legally, whatever their ages, this is the birthparents'
decision. Parents of a 14-year-old parent-to-be may feel
they should have a part in deciding whether this grandchild
is to be part of their family or will be reared by a different
family. It's a difficult time for them.

Talking with a good counselor is a good plan for your
parents, too, even if they're sure now, before birth, that
adoption is the best plan. When they first see their beautiful
grandchild, their feelings may take over. Just as this time
right after birth is not a good time for you to make a life-
changing decision, neither is it wise for your parents to
change their minds suddenly.

## Making the Final Decision

Sometimes the baby's mother and/or the father make an
adoption plan during pregnancy, then change their minds in
the hospital. When they see their baby, they feel instant
love. How, then, can they possibly release this child to
someone else to rear?

*It's a good idea to write down the reasons
for deciding on adoption.*

It's best to stall a couple of days before either finalizing
the adoption plan or deciding to parent the child themselves. After going through labor and delivery, the mother
probably finds it hard to make this life-changing decision.
At the moment, she "knows" she can't let her baby go.

If an adoption plan is made during pregnancy, it's a good
idea to write down the reasons for deciding on adoption.
Those reasons probably haven't changed now that the baby
is born. If the mother (and father) can remind themselves of
these reasons for adoption, they may be better able after
delivery to make a decision with which they can live.

It's all right if they change their minds. The final adoption decision can't be made before delivery. In some states,
independent adoptions are not finalized until several
months to a year after the child is placed with the adoptive
family.

The point is that deciding to place or not to place one's
child for adoption must not be done on the spur of the
moment. Either way, it's a terribly important decision for
the birthparents and for their child.

## Birthparents Will Grieve

Placing a baby for adoption is undoubtedly one of the
hardest things anyone can do. Any birthparent who carries
out an adoption plan needs to realize that s/he will probably
grieve intensely for this child s/he already loves.

*I signed the papers and Arnie was gone. For three
months we cried and we wondered — did we do the
right thing?*

*Sometimes I wish we hadn't, that we could have
raised him — and of course we could have — but we
had to think of his future. Not that I think material
things are so important, but the support of two
parents matters to us.*

*After a few months, it gets a little easier to handle.
It takes a lot of work to get past the grieving, and I
don't think you ever really get over it. Arnie is in the
back of my mind all the time. I think of him a lot.*

Birthparents should plan to continue seeing their counselor for awhile after their child is placed with the adoptive
parents. In fact, this is the time when counseling may be
especially needed. Joining a support group of young
birthparents may also be helpful.

## Supporting an Adoption Plan

*When I told my grandmother, she didn't know I
was so far along because I wasn't showing. She
wanted me to get an abortion, but I couldn't. I talked
to a counselor about open adoption, but I thought that
would be too hard.*

*When I saw other girls raising their babies, it
looked easy. For me, though, it's too hard. If I were
starting all over again, I might consider adoption.*

                                        Elisa Marie, 15 - Delila, 9 months

If someone in your class or another friend is considering
an adoption plan for her baby, what can you do to help her?
Things that are *not* helpful include saying:

• How could you possibly give your baby away?

• You must not love your baby.

• No one who cares about her child would consider
  adoption.

Why would anyone make such thoughtless comments? Hearing these things would be very hurtful to a young person considering an adoption plan. Most often, people making these comments are simply thoughtless. They don't realize how hurtful they are to a person going through the pain of deciding how best to provide a satisfying life for her child.

Students in a class of pregnant teenagers were discussing adoption. "How can we support a student who considers this very difficult and unpopular decision?" asked the teacher. Lauren, pregnant at 17, replied with exceptional thoughtfulness and caring:

*Listen and understand her thoughts. If someone tells you she's thinking about adoption, always listen with an open mind. Don't put her down for thinking that way because everyone has the right to their own thoughts. Maybe you don't agree, but it's not up to you. Just understanding and listening is a lot of help.*

Deciding to let another family rear one's child is a tremendously difficult decision. For a pregnant teen not yet ready to parent, adoption may be the most loving choice. Having friends who support the young birthparent(s) throughout this difficult time is important.

*For more information about adoption, see **Pregnant? Adoption Is an Option** by Lindsay (Morning Glory Press).*

*Her baby will be here soon.*

# 7

# Preparing for Labor and Delivery

- Nine Months of Preparation
- Those Early Contractions
- Prepared Childbirth
- You Need a Coach
- Relaxation Techniques Help
- Premature Labor Signs
- Prepare a Birth Plan
- Labor — An Athletic Event

*Prepared childbirth helped. This was my first baby and I didn't know what to do. They showed us a lot of what happens, especially the delivery.*

Ynez, 16 - Lenny 4 months

*Prepared childbirth helped me with focusing and breathing. Both my parents were with me during delivery. My dad wasn't going in but I said, "Put that suit on and go," and he did.*

*Dad had never seen a birth before — he was real nervous. After Antoine got here, Dad wanted to hold him so bad he hardly let the nurse clean him up.*

Elysha, pregnant at 17

During the first few weeks of pregnancy, you were probably busy with all those decisions you had to make. Perhaps you had to deal with the emotional upheaval your pregnancy caused your family, your boyfriend, and yourself. At the same time, you've been coping with the many physical changes discussed in chapter 2.

By the time you feel your baby moving inside you, you'll probably begin to think about labor and delivery. People may have shared their labor and delivery stories with you. Hearing other people's stories can be helpful, but remember that each person's experience is unique.

## Nine Months of Preparation

Most of us want to know how we can have as good a birthing experience as possible. You can do a lot all through your pregnancy to help you and your baby work together for a good birth experience for both of you.

### Stepping Stones to Labor and Delivery

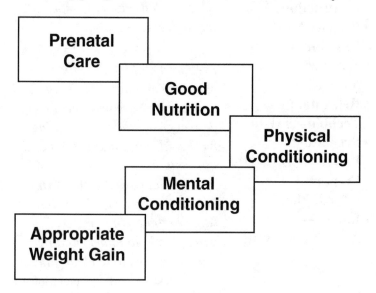

## Those Early Contractions

During the last few weeks of your pregnancy, your uterus will begin practicing for the big event.

---

**Uterus:** The hollow muscle
in which your baby is growing

---

You may feel early contractions. A contraction feels like your uterus is making a fist. You can see your belly get hard and move as your baby pushes it.

These early contractions are called Braxton-Hicks contractions or preterm or false labor. Sometimes people call them pains. Using this term, however, may make these sensations feel more like pain. The more you can relax and work with your baby now and when real labor begins, the less discomfort you're likely to feel.

When you get that first contraction, you may feel excited. You may even wonder if your baby will be born that day. You're likely, however, to have false labor on and off for several weeks. If you feel contractions three or more times in one hour, you should call your healthcare provider.

While some moms report that they don't experience these before-labor contractions, most do at least once or twice. The discomfort many mothers report may be partly related to getting uptight about this important work of their uterus and baby.

## Prepared Childbirth

*The prepared childbirth class helped me a lot. It showed me what to expect, how to breathe, and how to pace myself. And each time a contraction came, I concentrated on being calm. If you think it's going to be horrible, and the pain will be terrible, it will be a*

*lot worse. If you keep yourself calm and try to
concentrate, it's not as painful or as hard.*

Delia, 16 - Kelsey, 7 months

Prepared childbirth means just what it says — preparing
for childbirth. Prepared childbirth classes usually consist of
a series of meetings for parents-to-be. Purpose of the
meetings is to help the parents understand the process of
labor and delivery. The mother and father, the mother and
another helping person, or the single mother by herself
prepare for the birth of the child.

You'll learn what to expect in labor and how to cope
with the contractions and birth of your baby. Options for
pain relief will also be described.

Mothers and fathers who are prepared will understand
what is going on during labor and delivery. They will know
how to work with the contractions and the baby in order
to get their baby born as comfortably and safely as
possible.

*Prepared childbirth was a help because I knew
what was going to happen, and it didn't scare me so
much. It helped a lot with the breathing. Without it, I
think I would have panicked.*

Vicki, 17 - Deanne, 3 weeks

## You Need a Coach

*Prepared childbirth will help you understand
what's going on when you're going through labor and
delivery. My mom will be my coach. I feel better
about it now because I understand what will be
happening to me when my baby is born. My sister
can't believe I know so much about pregnancy. She
thinks I'm an expert.*

Marlene, 15 - 8 months pregnant

Check into the prepared childbirth classes in your area. You will be expected to take someone with you to your classes so that s/he can coach you during labor. Usually this person is the father of the baby.

> *Randy was there through delivery. I was in labor four days, and Randy would say, "Okay, calm down." He was my courage to go through it.*
>
> *He was real helpful with anything. He would help me get up from bed and walk me around. He was good about that. I was in active labor for four days, and I ended up with an emergency C-section.*
>
> Delia

If your baby's father either isn't around or he doesn't want to be involved in labor and delivery, ask someone else. Your mother, friend, even your father might make an excellent coach. The important point is that you get to a prepared childbirth class.

The coach plays an important role in prepared childbirth. S/he knows what's going on in your labor, and will be able to coach (tell you what to do) so you can cope better with the whole process. Most hospitals now allow the coach to be with the mother during delivery.

Prepared childbirth does not mean any one "method." Any one of several different methods may be used. Neither does prepared childbirth (sometimes called "natural" childbirth) mean you must endure whatever happens without the help of anesthesia. With adequate preparation, however, many women find they need very little help from drugs during labor and delivery.

There are three especially important reasons for taking a prepared childbirth class during pregnancy:

- The class will help you conquer fear of labor and delivery.

- You will learn about your body and what happens throughout pregnancy and delivery.

- You'll be able to share your childbirth experience with someone else — the person you choose to be your coach.

You'll also find you aren't out there all by yourself being pregnant. You'll meet other parents-to-be, and this is one place you can ask all your questions about childbirth.

*Every delivery is different. Don't listen to other people who say it hurts a lot because you don't know how you will do. I used to be scared listening to the other girls talk about their deliveries.*

*The exercises help you a lot. I used to do them while I watched TV at home.*

*Del used to take me to walk a lot. I'd get tired, but I'm glad he made me walk.*

Ynez

## Relaxation Techniques Help

*Everyone said labor is like having bad cramps, so I thought they would be these little cramps. But once they started coming, I thought I was going to die. But I didn't scream, I didn't make one sound. I remember falling asleep between contractions.*

*I was in labor for six or seven hours, and I told them when he was coming. With one push he was out.*
Camelia, 16 - Buchanan, 6 months

Apparently Camelia was able to relax enough to fall asleep between contractions. If you practice relaxation techniques at least twice each day, you can train yourself for labor. Remember, labor is just another name for work, and most of us need some training for a new job.

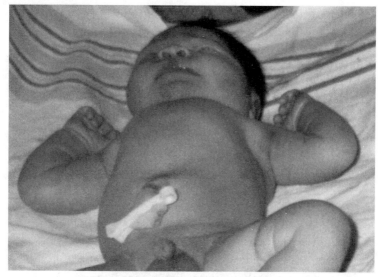

*Practicing relaxation techniques
helps you prepare for his birth.*

Relaxation is the most important technique you learn in childbirth class. When your muscles are relaxed, you and your baby get more oxygen and the contractions are less uncomfortable.

Some of these relaxation techniques are:

- **The Limp Noodle:** Tighten up all the muscles of your body and hold your breath for as long as you can. When you let your breath out, let go of all your muscles. Practice this two or three times each day for ten or fifteen minutes. You need to be able to do this automatically when you're in labor, and this will be hard if you haven't practiced.

- **The Focal Point:** Find something you like to look at (not a clock), something that you can see clearly from across the room. Look at it hard for a minute or two. At the same time, imagine your whole body is floating toward this focal point. Then take a deep breath and look away from the object.

Staying focused on an object throughout a contraction increases your concentration and helps you cope with the discomforts of labor.

- **Breathing:** Practice a long breath in through your nose, out through your mouth. This provides a maximum amount of oxygen for your body.

- **Touch Transfer:** Have someone rub your back. At the same time, have that person tell you how good this feels.

  Feeling those hands on your back and hearing a soothing voice during labor will help you be more relaxed. Somehow you can mentally transfer at least some of the pain to that person's hands. Even firm hand squeezes can help with this process.

- **Pelvic Rock:** Get down on the floor on your hands and knees. Arch your back up high like a cat. Then push your stomach toward the floor. Do this several times each day.

- **Kegels:** Kegels refer to the muscles you use when you urinate. Squeezing these muscles, then releasing them (as if you were going to start to urinate, then stop suddenly, then start again) helps prepare you for childbirth. Pretend you're in an elevator. Squeeze your way up to the tenth floor. Now come down again, stopping at every floor. Or count to 10 and release. Do this several times a day, but *not* while you're urinating.

- **Walking:** Walking several blocks each day is good for all your muscles. Just be sure to wear tennis shoes or other flat shoes. Going for a walk after lunch or dinner could mean less heartburn, too.

## Premature Labor Signs

You don't want to deliver your baby early even though being pregnant for nine months will seem like a long time. Babies born more than eight weeks early may have problems breathing, eating, and keeping warm. Your prenatal visits to your doctor or midwife are the best way to watch for any risk of preterm labor.

Signs that you might be starting preterm labor include:

• If your uterus contracts every ten minutes for at least an hour, even when you walk around *or* sit/lie still.

• You feel menstrual-like cramps in your lower abdomen.

• You have a low, dull backache below your waistline which may come and go or simply continue for some time.

• Pressure in your pelvis — a feeling that the baby is pushing down. You might have diarrhea at the same time. You might feel like you have the flu or very bad gas.

If any of these things happen three weeks or more before your due date, call your doctor or midwife right away. Also call if you have:

• Fluid coming from your vagina that is watery, mucousy, or slightly bloody.

• Blood from your vagina.

• A sudden increase in discharge from your vagina.

• A decrease or absence in fetal movement.

If you go to the hospital with any of these signs, the staff will check you to decide whether or not you're having preterm labor and make sure your baby is okay. If you are, they will probably give you medication to stop the labor. If you aren't in labor, you'll simply be sent home.

## Prepare a Birth Plan

The delivery of your baby is a big event. Planning for big events makes sense. Writing out a birth plan makes a lot of sense. Share your written plan with your coach, your partner, your healthcare providers, the admitting nurse, and the nurse in your labor room. Include:

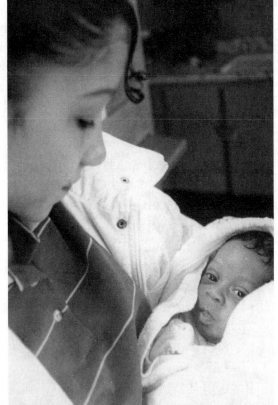

*Soon your baby will be in your arms.*

- Your medication preference.
- Persons you want to be with you during labor and birth.
- If you have a boy, do you want him circumcized?
- If you plan to breastfeed —
  - Immediately after birth? Or within first hour?
  - No bottle to be given baby.
- Baby in room with you — days? nights?
- Length of hospital stay (usually up to two days).

Remember this is a plan, how you hope your labor will progress. One thing that is predictable about labor is that no one knows how long it will take for your baby to be born. It's important to go with the flow and be flexible with your plan. Otherwise you might be set up for disappointment.

Visiting your hospital maternity center and seeing a labor/delivery room can be reassuring. You want to know something about this place where your baby will be born.

## Labor — An Athletic Event

Labor is an athletic event. Even if you haven't been into sports before, you'll star in this event. Just as athletes prepare every day, so should you do something daily to prepare your body and your mind for labor. Practice your relaxation and breathing in positions that feel comfortable to you such as the tub, shower, rocking chair, bed, or recliner.

It will be an athletic event for you, but your prize will be a little different. Your prize will be your baby.

*Be prepared!*

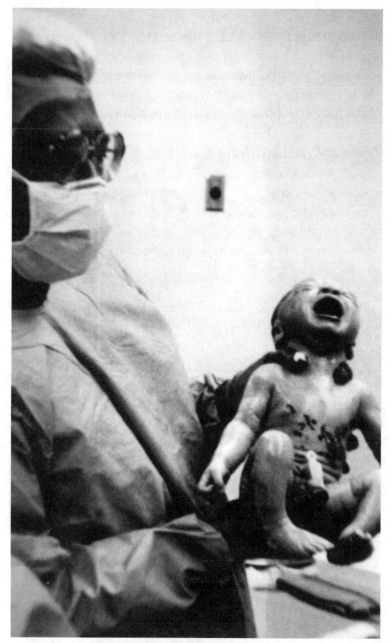

*He's ready to face life on the outside.*

# 8

# Your Baby
# Is Born

*Dan went in with me. I only had a three-hour labor, but it was real hard labor the whole time.*

*My water bag broke, and the next thing I knew, we were on our way to the hospital. It was at night, and I was almost three weeks overdue.*

*When I first saw Susie, I was happy. Then I got hungry.*

Cathi, 18 when Susie was born

*I was at the mall shopping for furniture. All of a sudden I felt this sharp pain that felt different, and then I felt wet. I went to the bathroom and checked. I wasn't sure it was my water bag because it was a very slow leak. Then I started feeling contractions, but I wasn't sure I was in labor.*

*My mother was with me, and we decided to go to the hospital. I thought they might send me home, but they said, "We'll keep you. You're in labor." And within half an hour, I had gone through transition. I was in labor a total of four hours.*

*I had an epidural. Once those pains started coming, I turned into a real baby. If you don't like pain, the epidural is wonderful. I was able to enjoy everything. I got an episiotomy which didn't hurt until the epidural wore off.*

Courtney, 15 - Ricky, 3 months

Hint: Ask your doctor or midwife at what point during the signs of early labor she wants you to call. What should you do if you go into labor when the office isn't open?

## Signs of Early Labor

Labor may be easier for you if you understand what is happening inside your body. Your uterus has several jobs to do before your baby is born. One of these jobs is the softening of your cervix.

**Cervix:** neck of your uterus

When you're not pregnant, your cervix is usually tightly closed. This is the reason your baby doesn't fall out during pregnancy.

As labor begins, your body releases hormones which tell your cervix to soften up and get out of the way. This process is referred to as *dilation*.

**Dilation:** opening

Both your vagina and your cervix become soft and stretchy during labor. This makes it possible for your baby to come out.

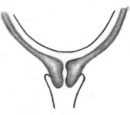

*Beginning dilation
(not active labor)*

During pregnancy, your cervix is sealed with a mucous plug. This plug keeps germs in the vagina from getting in the uterus, germs which could give your baby an infection. As your cervix starts to open, this plug comes out. It will be stringy, gooey, and clear or white with possibly a tinge of pink. This may be your first sign of labor. When it happens, call your healthcare provider.

Some people never notice the mucous plug. Their labor may begin with the rupture of the sack of amniotic water. This is the sack in which your baby has been growing.

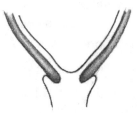

*Mid-labor
(Regular contractions)*

If this happens, you'll feel a gush of warm water. If it's amniotic fluid, it will keep coming out no matter how much you try to hold it.

Other people have backaches and feel "heavy" when labor begins. Practicing your prepared childbirth techniques during this time will be helpful.

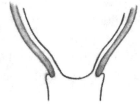

*End of labor
(Your baby is ready
for birth)*

## Timing Your Contractions

*My labor started at night. I couldn't sleep — about every 30 minutes I'd wake up and walk. Next morning, I wasn't feeling good, so I didn't go to school.*

*Later that day my contractions were getting closer.*
*By 10 p.m., they came about every seven minutes. My*
*mom said, "Do you want to go to the hospital?"*

*I said, "Not yet." Then I lay down, and the con-*
*tractions came every five minutes. At midnight I told*
*my dad to take me to the hospital. I could barely walk*
*by then, and the nurse took me in a wheelchair to*
*a room.*

*They put two belts on my stomach, one to measure*
*the heartbeat of the baby, and one for the*
*contractions.*

*The contractions got stronger, and two hours later,*
*I had Duwayne. It didn't hurt as much as I expected.*

Shalonda, 16 - Duwayne, 2 months

When your contractions start, have someone time them.
How far apart are they? Count the time from the beginning
of one contraction to the beginning of the next contraction.
This is the *interval.*

How long do they continue? Count the time from the
beginning of the contraction to the end of it. This is the
*duration.*

If this is real labor, your contractions won't go away.
Your doctor will want to know both the interval and
duration of your contractions.

## Pain Relief Medication

*My mom and Julio were there the whole time. First*
*I'd squeeze Julio's hand, then my mom's.*

*When I was three centimeters, my doctor asked if I*
*wanted pain medication. All through my pregnancy I*
*had said I wouldn't have anything, but now I told him*
*I wanted the strongest thing he had.*

*He gave me an epidural, and I was out for two*

*hours. Then I started feeling everything again. The
contractions were coming and coming and coming. I
was in labor for 23 hours.*

*I was eight centimeters, and I wanted to push, but
the nurse kept saying, "You can't push yet." I wanted
to push so bad, but if I had, I guess the cervix would
have swelled, and it would have been even harder.*

*Finally she told me to push. I was pushing and
thinking, "Oh my God, this thing is never coming
out." But I pushed once, and that's all it took. Elena
came out.*

Monica, pregnant at 14

You may want to talk to your doctor about pain relief
during labor. Find out about your choices *before* your labor
begins. Even if you're sure you don't want drugs during
labor and/or delivery, you should know about your options.
It's easier to understand your choices when you're not
already in labor. With or without medication, you can
expect a fine healthy baby.

Pain killers are given either through the IV or with a shot
to your hip.

---

**IV (Intravenous):** Method of giving medicine
by inserting a needle into the vein,
usually in the arm.

---

These drugs can dull some of the pain, but it also goes
through the placenta to the baby. It may cause the baby to
become sleepy, and it can slow labor down. You may want
to ask your healthcare provider if she uses this drug or any
others during labor.

The most commonly used anesthesia is the epidural.
This is a process in which the anesthesiologist places a soft
rubber catheter in the lower back. A medication similar to

what a dentist uses to lessen dental pain is then injected.
This causes numbness from below the umbilicus (belly
button) down into the legs. If this is given to you, a fetal
monitor is likely to be used, too.

The fetal monitor is a device for measuring how long,
how hard, and how often contractions come. It also keeps
track of the baby's pulse and breathing. It looks like a
paddle, and is fastened on with a belt. It doesn't hurt.

## Transition Stage

*I started getting the pains Saturday night, about 15
to 20 minutes apart. By 11 p.m. they started coming
three to five minutes apart. We went to the hospital at
midnight, but I was only dilated three centimeters.
About 1:15 the doctor broke my water bag.*

*The contractions were coming faster and harder.
At 3:30 they gave me a shot of demerol and I felt a lot
better.*

*The demerol wore off in a couple of hours, and the
contractions were closer and harder than ever and
hurting even more.*

*Finally they gave me some more demerol. They
checked me at 7:15 a.m., and I was dilated to a little
more than nine centimeters. The next thing I knew the
doctor gave me a shot to numb me for my episiotomy.
Then they told me to push.*

Alice Ann, 15 - Vincent, 3 weeks

The last period of labor is called *transition*. This begins
when the cervix is seven centimeters dilated. During this
period (15-60 minutes) the baby moves down into the birth
canal and prepares to come out. When the head of the baby
can be seen, it is described as *crowning* — what a lovely
word! Someone important is coming — your baby.

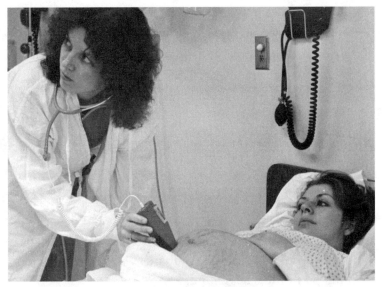

*"Yes, she's really in labor."*

Your doctor or midwife will stay with you now until your baby is born. When your cervix is completely dilated, she'll tell you to push when you feel the urge to do so. This feeling is the same as the urge to have a bowel movement. Pushing too soon can cause the cervix to swell and slow things down. It also puts more pressure on baby's head.

It may take about five pushes to bring your baby into the world. Many mothers say this is the most exciting part of the whole process. At the very least, you know that your labor is ending.

As the time for delivery gets nearer, the doctor may perform an episiotomy.

---

**Episiotomy:** a small cut to enlarge the vaginal opening

---

If you've had medication injected, you won't feel this cut. Actually, you may not feel it even if you don't have medication. Nature provides some numbness in this area.

## Your Baby's Arrival

*I pushed for about ten minutes, and I heard my
baby crying. My aunt was saying, "He's so pretty.
Look at all his hair." He didn't look too pretty. He
was all purple.*

*They cleaned him up and brought him back to me. I
fell in love like never before. He had the fattest little
cheeks and so much hair, and his thumb was in
his mouth.*

Alice Ann

As delivery nears, you may feel shivery, and they'll put
warm blankets over your legs and body. It isn't really cold,
it's just a hormonal shift that prepares you for the most
exciting part of this adventure.

If you want to watch, be sure to tell the nurse/doctor to
adjust the mirror for you. If you wear glasses, you may
want to request them. I (Jeanne L.) missed seeing the birth
of one of my children because I wasn't wearing my glasses.
I simply couldn't see in the mirror clearly.

After you're in position, the doctor will wash the
birthing area. Your baby's progress will be watched carefully, and they will be checking your baby's heart rate
often. Don't be alarmed by this concern. It's all part of
making sure things are going well for both of you.

The crowning is part of the baby's descent from your
body into her own world. The head slips out of your body
and turns to the side. (Some films about delivery make it
look like the doctor turns the head, but it's the baby
who turns.)

The shoulders now come out one at a time. When the
second shoulder comes out, the rest of the body emerges
quickly. This all happens within a few minutes.

This ends the second stage of labor. Your baby is born.

*I thought everything would be hard in the hospital. I was all worried about what I would do when s/he came out. But it was a beautiful day. It's beautiful to see your baby come out of her vagina. I cut his umbilical cord, and as soon as they'd checked him, they let me hold him.*

Del, 20 - Lenny, 4 months

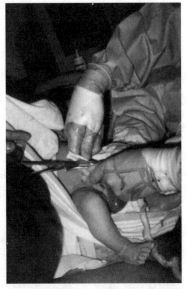

*"I cut his umbilical cord."*

Usually you'll see your baby right away. You'll feel lots of excitement as you find out the gender and condition of your new person. Some babies cry immediately, and some need to have mucous or amniotic fluid removed from their airway before they begin to cry. The nurse will gently remove the mucous and amniotic fluid with a bulb syringe. This doesn't hurt the baby.

*I got to see Keonia right after she was pulled out. They put her on my belly for a little while before she was taken to be cleaned up.*

*She was long and skinny and was better looking than I had expected. She was warm, wet, slippery, and there was a smell — not a bad scent at all. To me, it was a sweet scent.*

Lei, 16 - Keonia, 4 months

*When the doctor told me to push, Caelin was out with four pushes. My husband was crying. He was so happy because when the nurse got Caelin, she started crying. When the nurse handed her to Doug, Caelin*

*stopped crying. He used to talk to her in my stomach,
so she already knew him.*

Alaina, 17 - Caelin, 4 months

## Delivery of the Placenta

Next on the agenda is your body's completion of the
birth process. The placenta has nourished your baby for
nearly nine months. It now needs to end its service by
separating from your uterine wall and coming out. This
happens within 15 minutes of delivery. One or two
menstrual-like cramps and out it comes.

Your doctor will then repair your episiotomy, if you
have one, by putting in a few stitches. Large sanitary
napkins are put on you. You will have heavy period-like
flow of blood for a few days. Occasionally a blood clot will
come out, too. These are from the area where the placenta
separated from the uterus. If, after a few days, the bleeding
is still bright red, call your healthcare provider.

During this flow time do not use tampons. The tissue is
so soft the tampon could go up high in the vagina and
you'd have a problem getting it out. An infection could
then develop and cause you to be quite sick.

You may go to a recovery room if you have had
anesthesia. Or you may go to a regular room for the remaining time you'll spend at the hospital. Often mothers
think they would like to go home right away. However, a
few hours of sleep and a little practice feeding your baby
will make it easier when you do go home.


## The Circumcision Decision

Some boy babies are circumcised soon after birth. This
is an operation in which the loose folds of skin at the end of
the penis are cut off by the doctor.

Before a baby can be circumcised, parents must sign a

*Grandma and Grandpa meet their grandson.*

consent form. Before delivery, parents should decide, if they have a boy, whether or not they want him to be circumcised. Some medical research shows that uncircumsized men may be more likely to have STIs which could affect them in adulthood. Others say it is an unnecessary operation, that it hurts the baby, and therefore should not be done. In fact, baby boys today are less likely to be circumcised than was the case a generation ago.

> *I didn't have Buchanan circumcised. His father isn't circumcised, and I think circumcision is unnecessary pain. It hurts them, and I think it traumatizes them. All you have to do is teach them to pull back the skin and clean it.*
>
> Camelia, 16 - Buchanan, 6 months

Sometimes deciding whether or not to have a son circumcised depends on the family's religious, ethnic, and/or cultural background.

Some parents decide to circumcise or not to circumcise depending on whether the father has had this operation. They think their son might be more comfortable if he "matched" his father. Others think it is important for their son to look like the other boys around him. If most boys in their community are being circumcised, he will be, too.

## For Some, a C-Section

For about twenty percent of moms, a Caesarean section is necessary.

---

**Caesarean section (C-section):** Delivery of child by cutting through walls of mom's abdomen.

---

Delia was in that twenty percent needing a C-section. Her labor didn't progress as she expected:

*About 11 a.m. I started contractions. They were every three minutes, and they came out of the blue. They were in my back, then would come to my front.*

*They checked me, and the contractions got stronger and stronger — two minutes apart. My doctor checked me. He said I wasn't dilating yet, and my water bag hadn't broken, so he said we had to stop the labor. He gave me a shot, and the contractions slowed down and weren't as bad.*

*He checked me at 6:30 p.m. that day. He said I still hadn't started to dilate, and that I should go home. So I went home at midnight.*

*The next morning the contractions kept coming, and they were strong. At 10 a.m. I had finished taking a shower, and I was dressed. I was blow-drying my hair when all of a sudden all this water gushed down my legs. I thought, "God, am I wetting myself without feeling it?"*

*So I changed clothes and put on another pair of pants. It happened again. They rushed me to the hospital, but by that time, my contractions had stopped.*

*They started again, so I called Randy and said, "This is it." He rushed over to the hospital, and he was all happy. My contractions were strong, and the nurse made me walk around for a couple of hours.*

*Then I checked into the birthing center, but I still wasn't dilating. They started shooting stuff into me, and within an hour my contractions were so painful and so close I could barely catch my breath between them.*

*The nurse came in and rushed me to the other side of the hospital. The doctor said my baby was in danger, and he had to do a C-section. They gave me an epidural, and I started feeling better. Kelsey started to cry immediately when they lifted her out.*

*I started to shake, and my temperature went up to 104°. I stayed awake just long enough to see Randy holding Kelsey and saying, "I've got a daughter. I've got a daughter."*

Delia, 16 - Kelsey, 7 months

Being told during labor that she must have a C-section is usually disappointing to a young woman. Liz shares her experience:

*When he said I had to have a C-section, I broke out in tears. I was scared. I didn't want one.*

*First they put the IV in, and they got me prepped and ready. They shaved my stomach including the top pubic hair. Then when they moved me to the delivery room they put the epidural in my back.*

*I couldn't feel them cut, but when they pulled her*

*out I could feel it. I'm lying there and have a curtain
in front of me. I heard him cry, and my mom said,
"It's a boy."*

*And I said, "Does he have all of his fingers and
toes?"*

*Then I asked the nurse what his Apgar score was,
and she said, "What do you want it to be?"*

*I said "Ten."*

*She said, "How about 9.9?"*

*It happened so fast. I was so tired I couldn't even
keep my eyes open. I hadn't slept for a long time. I
stayed in the hospital for four days, and I healed
pretty fast. I was sitting up and walking around the
next day. But when I came home, I was real tired.*

Liz, 16 - Jonathan, 3 months

Reasons a mom might have a C-section include:
1) Cephalopelvic disproportion — the baby is too big
   in comparison with the mother's size.
2) Labor slows down or stops.
3) Certain types of infections.
4) Placenta previa (placenta covers inner cervix).
5) Fetal distress.
6) Breech (bottom first) or transverse (sideways)
   position of the baby.

Doctors used to feel that when a mom had one C-section,
all her later babies would have to be delivered that way,
too. Now we know that if the condition that caused the first
C-section isn't present during a later pregnancy, she may be
able to deliver vaginally.

## Baby's First Test

Your baby's responses will be measured and noted with
something called the *Apgar score* one minute after birth,

again at five minutes, again at 15 minutes. Scores range from 0 to 10. It's usually a little better at each measurement because baby's color generally improves with time.

The Apgar test measures the color, pulse, cry, movements and strength of breathing. If comments are made about these things by the doctor and nurse, don't feel worried. It's normal for them to be watchful.

Your baby will be weighed and measured, washed, and wrapped in a blanket. The nurse will then either take your baby to the nursery or give her back to you. Most hospitals try to keep you and baby together as much as possible.

If you're breastfeeding, plan to nurse your baby within the first hour after her birth. A nurse will help you get started. Ask your doctor or midwife to make sure the hospital doesn't give your baby a bottle at all. See chapter 11 for more information on breastfeeding.

Going home is something fathers often find an especially exciting event. Maybe they feel fatherly responsibility around that time. Being in charge of mom and baby makes them more aware of their part in this new life.

For each of you, going home is the beginning of your new adventure.

*When we came home I felt different. This was something new. I had to start my life all over again, learning who comes first, and trying to get all the sleep I could. I had to get used to another person, a very loud person you can't ignore, somebody I had to attend to the minute he opened his mouth. My life was changed forever.*

Elysha, 21 - Antoine, 4

*For more information, see **All About Pregnancy: A Complete Guide to a Prepared Birth from Pregnancy to Parenthood** by Ginny Brinkley, et al. (Avery Publishing)*

*All babies love to read with Mom.*

# 9

# Babies with Special Needs

*I was only 30 weeks pregnant when Casey was born. He weighed 3 pounds, 5 ounces, and he had to stay in the hospital for five weeks. When he came home he was 4 pounds, 11 ounces. He was pretty healthy for being so little, but he had to stay in the hospital to learn how to suck and to keep his body temperature even.*

*Going home without him was strange. You'd think after you have a baby you'd bring it home with you and start taking care of him. I visited him in the hospital every day, and I'd spend several hours with him. He had the IV in his arm, and he had little monitors on him. To feed him, they would put a tube down his throat. Once he learned how to suck, they didn't need to do that any more.*

*I pumped my breasts all the time he was in the hospital. I would take the milk down there and they'd put it in freezers, and feed it to him. I wanted to get him out of the real critical stage when he was in the hospital, and I knew breast milk would be better. I hadn't planned to breastfeed, but I knew it would be better for him. He was so tiny he needed all the help he could get.*

*He's been very healthy since he came home.*

Charity, 17 - Casey, 18 months

For a small number of parents, the arrival of their long-awaited baby may bring with it special new challenges. It may be a short-term problem. Casey's mom couldn't take him to school or out with people generally for six months, but now at eighteen months, Casey is a healthy little boy.

Some babies have far greater needs than Casey. When a baby is born with a special need, parents may need to make some adjustments in their plans and their dreams for their child.

---

**Special Needs Baby:** A child with mild, moderate, or severe disability.

---

Less than one percent of babies are identified during the first few weeks as having moderate or severe special needs. Some of the causes of these conditions are:

- Very low birthweight, below two pounds.
- Prematurity, especially earlier than 25 weeks.
- Genetic changes causing conditions such as Down Syndrome (DS), cerebral palsy (CP), and others.

- Lack of oxygen to the baby's brain during development or during labor and delivery.
- Drug and alcohol use by the mother during pregnancy.
- Infections including sexually transmitted diseases.
- Other unknown causes.

## How Parents Feel

*After delivery I asked my mom, "Where is he?" My mom told me he was premature, and they took him to another hospital.*

*That afternoon, my boyfriend walked in and he started to cry. He said, "Our baby is sick." Then he told me Enrique had Down Syndrome.*

*I thought, Why me, why did this happen to me?*

*When I came home from the hospital nobody wanted to leave me alone. I always had someone there. I was never alone, and that was good because I didn't have much time to think about it. When I did have time to think about it I prepared myself. I talked with my mom, I cried with my mom. I have a big family and they have all supported me.*

*I'm starting to go to programs to learn more about Down Syndrome. They said it's mostly older women. Sometimes I tell myself he doesn't seem like he has Down's.*

*He's not a severe case. It's really up to me to teach him what he needs to know. Two therapists have been here, one from the Regional Center, and the other one was a nurse who came to check up on him.*

*At first Edwardo was upset, it was hard, and we agreed we had to stick together in order to raise Enrique. Edwardo loves Enrique to death. He spoils him. He takes him everywhere and so do I. We tell everybody. We aren't ashamed of it.*

*Enrique is always smiling. He likes me to sing to him. He acts like he sings to me back. He's real smart. For Down Syndrome, he's real smart.*

*I think what has also helped me be okay is that I have a good family that has supported me. My mom is my love.*

Carla, 18 - Enrique, 5 months

Most parents who are told their baby has a special need find it hard to believe at first. Once the fact sinks in that something really could be wrong, many parents become eager to find a cure for the problem. Others try to find out why, and even occasionally want to blame someone for what has happened. All these feelings are natural, but problems can arise between a couple when one partner blames the other for the baby's condition. Other parents become depressed.

What seems to help with these feelings is to talk them over with a person who has facts about the baby's condition. That could be your doctor, a nurse, the social worker at the hospital, your priest, minister, rabbi, imam, or other spiritual adviser. It could be a person from one of the many public and private community agencies who help families with special babies. If your baby should have special needs, don't be afraid to ask for help in understanding what has happened.

*When Montana was in the intensive care nursery I was so afraid to even touch him because he was so small. The nurses and therapists helped me there, but when it was time to take him home, I was really scared. My mother asked if a nurse would come visit us. They said they'd check.*

*Danny was upset and said we could do it ourselves.*

*When we left the hospital, we ran away for awhile.*
*Our baby got worse because he didn't get some treat-*
*ments he needed. I wish we'd listened to the doctor.*

Nancy, 19 - Montana, 6 months

## Helping Baby with Special Needs

*Parenting a Down Syndrome baby takes a lot of*
*patience. You need to understand what DS is. If you*
*don't know what it is, you'll expect too much from the*
*baby. In reality, you get what he can do.*

Carla

Recently we've been hearing on television and in the
newspapers about the importance of early brain development. It's very important for *all* children from the earliest
moments of life to have experiences that help them grow.
They need to feel loved as they learn about the world
around them.

This is especially true for babies with special needs.
They may need extra help to experience the things other
babies get on their own. Like all babies, they need to have
their mother and other special people in their lives pay
attention to them.

Often a long intensive care stay at the hospital or simply
physical weakness makes it hard for the baby to respond in
the usual way to those whom they love. These babies are
often described as "really good" or "very easy" because
they don't cry often.

They also may not smile and get excited when their
loved person comes near. When the baby acts like that, the
mother doesn't know she needs to keep trying so the baby
will learn to do these things, to smile and get excited.

*All* babies learn. Those with special needs just learn at a
different speed than typical babies.

There are many kinds of specialists who can help parents figure out just what their individual baby needs to progress. For information about people in your area, talk to the doctor or medical social worker at the hospital where you delivered. They will help you find the best people in your community.

Many kinds of services for children with special needs are available free of cost, but a family needs to be connected to the agency that pays for these services. Some of the kinds of specialists are:

- Service coordinator — a specially trained person who helps find the best type of service for you and your child in your community.

- Physical/occupational therapist — specially trained to help with exercises for strength, feeding needs, positions that help baby do things more easily.

- Home nurse — helps parent or other caregiver learn how to give baby medicine, use special equipment, and recognize the baby's cues about when she is happy or when she needs help.

- Early intervention teacher — helps the family understand the early development of their baby. The teacher also suggests activities to help the baby learn more.

## Telling Others About Baby

*In a way I wonder, what do people think? Nobody knows why DS happens. But I think, what are they going to think? What did she do in her pregnancy? But now I don't çare what anybody thinks. If people say retarded, I don't really like it. God made him special.*

*I think it might get harder when he gets older. That's when it will hit me because I will see him different from other kids. Right now he's like other babies. I'm scared for him because he will wonder why he is different.*

Carla

Parents may find it hard to tell their family and friends about their baby's special needs. It's best to give the correct information to as many family members as you can.

It's all right to cry. It's also all right for grandparents to cry.

Parents need to share the information they have, especially the cause of the condition if they know. For many friends, this may be the first time they have known anyone with a special need. They may offer advice or suggest solutions the parent doesn't like. Usually these comments come because they sincerely want to help. If this happens to you, practice either in your head or with your partner how you might answer them.

"We have a plan to get help for our baby."

"We love him very much and accept him as he is."

"We were shocked, too, at first, but we're getting used to the idea."

*When my mother-in-law heard about the cerebral palsy, she said I must have done drugs. I didn't, and when I told the nurse at the hospital about it, she told me that isn't what causes it. I felt much better, and I told Tom to tell his mother.*

Lisa, 18 - Cherie, 14 months

## Helping Friend with Special-Needs Child

*I haven't had one friend call me and say "Congratulations." Nobody has called me to ask how he is. I have only one friend who plays with him and holds him.*

*What hurts is that they couldn't call me and say,
"Congratulations, you have a baby." If you hear it
from someone else, why not call me? If they were
friends, they would call.*

Carla

Many parents of children with special needs are hurt
because their friends don't talk with them as much as they
did. Sometimes they seem afraid to talk about or touch
the baby.

*When Omar was born with a cleft palate, Josh and
I cried and didn't know what to do. At first I was
worried that I'd done something to make this happen.*

*We felt better after we talked with the surgeon. He
told us what he could do, and that this wouldn't mean
Omar would be handicapped for life.*

*My friends didn't want to see him, and that hurt the
most. After a while, Josh and I never took him out. I
felt like I had a handicap, too.*

Luz, 18 - Omar, 4 months

If you know someone whose baby has a special need, try
to treat him or her the same as you did before. It's all right
to ask questions about the baby. You can ask the usual
questions, like, "Does he sleep all night yet?"

You can also ask other questions related to his special
condition. "How do you feed a baby with a cleft palate?"

Ask to hold the baby. Admire the same qualities you
would in any baby. "What big eyes he has!" or "She has
such pretty skin." Invite your friend to come to school and
participate in other activities she would normally do. Her
life isn't over because she has a baby with special needs.

Avoid:

• Giving advice unless you really know something

helpful, such as who to call to get information.

* Telling stories about others who have had unhappy outcomes due to disability.

* Using words that you may have heard or used when you were younger such as "retard," "moron," and others. Discourage others from using them, too.

## Things to Remember

If you have a child with special needs, accept help from family, friends, and professionals. *All children* develop at their own rates, but they do develop. As a parent, you are the most important person in your child's life. You will need to help your child grow and get the things s/he needs.

> *When the doctor told us our baby had Down Syndrome we didn't know what he meant. The baby looked so cute to us and nobody else thought anything could be wrong. After he told us more, I cried, but Jerry said he still didn't believe it. He wanted the doctor to do more tests.*
>
> Celeste, 17 - Jeremy, 7 months

Stay in touch with friends who have made you feel comfortable about all that has happened. Share the care and development of your child with your partner and family.

If your friend has a child with special needs, stay friends. Be a good listener. Treat your friend like any other friend who has just had a new baby. Include your friend in the usual activities of life.

Encourage her by noticing how well she is doing the new things expected of her. Tell her how impressed you are with her ability to work with and enjoy her child. Offer practical help such as transportation, information, babysitting, and simply being there for her.

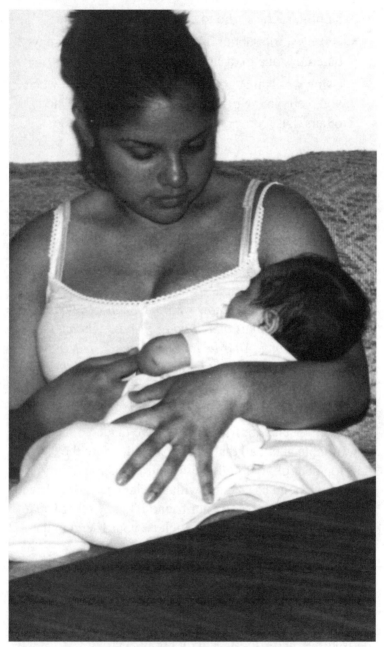

*Your fourth trimester — and baby is finally here.*

# 10

# Your
# Fourth Trimester

*I'm happy I had a baby, but during that first week I said, "Oh God, I shouldn't have had this baby." But after the first week, Joe started helping. And I suppose it was after-baby blues, too.*

Rosita, 18 - Jenny, 4 weeks

*Coming home with Blair was weird, real different. I didn't know what to do. In the hospital the nurses did everything so when I got home I was really scared. I got help at first, but then everybody had to go back to school or work, and I was home alone. It was hard to believe I had a baby.*

Brooke, 18 - Blair, 3 months

## How Will You Feel?

You may be surprised at how easily you get tired during
the first few days after you deliver your baby. Your fatigue
is a combination of the after-effects of labor, your lack of
sleep because of your baby's frequent feeding, and the
hormonal changes your body experiences after delivery.

*That first week I'd fall asleep and I'd hear a baby
— and I thought it was still in my stomach. Then I'd
finally wake up and Lenny was crying. So I'd get up
and fix his bottle and feed him.*

Ynez, 16 - Lenny, 4 months

Remember the tiredness of early pregnancy that was
caused by hormone changes? Now those hormones are
changing back.

*When we left the hospital we went straight to my
boyfriend's mom's house because she wanted us there
because his dad was coming over. There were lots of
people, and I was so tired.*
*They took pictures, but I didn't smile or anything. I
just wanted to go to sleep and relax.*

Emilia, 17 - Sancia, 6 months

Your stitches may hurt for a few days. You'll be having
some bleeding for about two weeks, and the color will go
from red to pink to brown to yellow to white. Sometimes
new moms feel so good they start vacuuming, lifting, etc. If
bleeding goes back to red, slow down! If it's bright red, call
your doctor. Use napkins rather than tampons to care for
the bleeding after delivery, as explained in chapter 8.

It's a good idea to continue taking your prenatal vitamins, especially if you're breastfeeding. This will help you
avoid anemia and speed your recovery.

You may notice changes in your temperature as your

hormones change gears. If you feel sick as well, be sure to check your temperature. Sometimes a mom has an infection and needs to call the doctor.

And remember, no matter how well you're feeling, be sure you see your healthcare provider for your postpartum checkup. This is usually scheduled four to six weeks after delivery. As mentioned later in this chapter, it's wise not to attempt sexual intercourse until after this appointment.

## After-Baby Blues

*When I went home, after two days in the hospital, it was very overwhelming. I was very tired, no motivation. I didn't want to take care of Clancy. I was crying all the time. I still have the baby blues. I find myself crying over stupid little things.*

*I couldn't believe I had a baby. I would kind of close my eyes and wish he would disappear. I knew he was here to stay, but the shock of being a mother was so overwhelming. I couldn't believe it.*

Chelsea, 19 - Clancy, 2 months

*After Kamie was born it was hard. I had been through the classes and thought I knew everything, but for two weeks, I felt depressed.*

*It went away in two weeks, but during that time I didn't want to hold Kamie, I didn't even want her. During those whole two weeks Lucas would get up with her and feed her and change her. She's daddy's little girl now.*

Kelsey, 19 - Kamie, 21 months

A lot of mothers are unhappy at least part of the time during the first week or two. To make things worse, a young mother may think she *should* be delighted. This baby for whom she waited so long is finally here. So why isn't she thrilled?

*Don't get upset when he cries. Andrea used to hate it. If Dennis cried for a whole minute, she'd be crying, too. That first day she was trying to change him, get him dressed, feed him—and he wouldn't shut up for anything.*

Ted, 18 - Dennis, 2 months

*Each time Elaine cried, I cried. Not being able to get back in my clothes bothered me, too. I was pretty depressed from the day I came home with Elaine until she was about three months old. Then I started being a little happier, calmer about things. I was only 16 then. With Susan, I haven't had much depression.*

Maya, 21 - Elaine, 5; Susan, 7 weeks

Many mothers (50-80 percent) get these after-baby blues. Realizing how much work a baby takes and how tied down she is with this tiny helpless creature are two of the reasons she feels sad.

*Mother needs to sleep when baby does.*

But she also has a physical reason. Her body is adjusting to being non-pregnant. As your hormones work hard to "get over" your nine months of pregnancy, you may feel pretty mixed up at times.

## Getting Help

*Today was a rough day. She's been a grouch the whole day. Last night she was even worse.*

*I try feeding her, changing her, singing to her, and nothing seems to work. I just don't understand what she needs.*

*Sometimes I feel like I'm going crazy. I think I need time to myself because I haven't had that in awhile. These past few days have been hard. I haven't gotten anything done. I don't even have time for my work.*

Marlene, 15 - Evan, 3 weeks

The best cure for after-baby blues is to get some help with baby care and to take some time to do things you want to do for yourself. If you can, get away from the house, go to the mall or a movie for a couple of hours. You'll feel much better.

I (Jean B.) remember my mother advising me to sleep when my baby slept, and that really helped me. It also helps a lot to talk to someone. Don't keep those unhappy feelings all bottled up!

*My mom works and I had all these things to get done. I had to get food stamps, find a job, get childcare assistance. And everybody wants to see her. Plus there's laundry, bottles to be washed . . .*

Karry, 17 - Abijah, 5 weeks

Remember, too, that you can get help for many problems. You are entitled to finish school. You may be eligible for food stamps and financial aid.

Call your teacher, doctor, nurse or social worker to find
out about job training, daycare services, church programs,
social programs, or other support opportunities in your
community.

If you have just had a baby, and you feel sad even as you
look at your beautiful infant, remember that you're not
weird. You're perfectly normal, and you'll probably feel
better soon.

If this low feeling lasts for more than two weeks, it may
be more serious. Do check with your healthcare provider
about other kinds of help.

## Lifestyle Changes

*I can't do the things I used to do like go to the
beach. I have to stay home with the baby. I'm not as
free as I used to be. I have to wash clothes and make
formula.*

*I don't get as many calls from my friends as I used
to. That bothers me. I like to shop and I can't go
shopping as much. I'm not dating because I have to
be with Chandra all the time.*

*Sometimes I want to go someplace. I get ready to
go, and then . . . suddenly I see the baby there beside
me. I've just forgotten her!*

Maria, 18 - Chandra, 6 weeks

Often a teenage mother — any mother and most fathers,
for that matter — finds caring for a tiny baby changes her
style of living a great deal. If you're breastfeeding, you're
entirely responsible for feeding your baby. You may feel
you're doing nothing much but feeding her those first few
days. See chapter 11 for more on breastfeeding.

As your baby matures, you'll be able to include her in
some of your activities. Life may never again be quite as
simple and carefree for you — no more deciding on the

spur of the moment to take off for the beach or the river. Even shopping with a small child is complicated. But with extra planning, it can be done.

*My lifestyle is entirely different. Before, I could just get up and leave and do things on instinct. But now we have to plan ahead and take about an hour getting ready to go.*

*You plan your life, too — she's with you so your life has to be different. Especially money — you can't just be spending your money on anything you want now.*

Cheryl, 16 - Racquelle, 2 months

*My girlfriends used to ask me to go with them. They used to call me when he was about two weeks old, and they'd say, "Let's go out and have a good time."*

*I'd say, "I can't because I have to take care of Eric." They called again and again for about a month, but then they stopped. They knew I couldn't go out with them.*

*They come over to see me, and they talk about parties and stuff. Then they look at me and say, "I'm sorry," because they're talking about it in front of me. But I don't mind. When Eric's older, he can go with me some places if there isn't drinking and pot.*

Jeanne, 16 - Eric, 2 months

## Bonding with Your Baby

*After we went home, I would carry him all the time, and when he would sleep, I'd just stand over him and stare at him. I couldn't believe that he came out of me. He was the most beautiful little creature I've ever seen. In the hospital I didn't even want to sleep, I was so excited.*

Camelia, 18 - Buchanan, 6 months

Bonding with your baby means falling in love. It has all the same ups and downs about it. Anybody who has ever fallen in love with anyone knows sometimes the person you love the most can make you terribly angry as well as lift your spirits remarkably. This can be true of your baby.

Sometime during the first two months you should feel this surge of love, that this baby is truly yours. Some people experience these feelings more strongly than others. If a mother's life isn't going as well as she'd like, she may not bond as easily with her baby.

Feeding your baby yourself, holding your baby, talking with other people about your beautiful child, and showing your baby off to others all help this falling-in-love-with-your-baby phenomenon.

## Handling Stress

*I remember nights when I just wanted to go crazy because I didn't know what to do.*

*Being alone is hard. I used to wish that Bob had just half the responsibility — just to let him have a baby for a week, for a night . . . but he was gone.*

*It was hard. I remember the times I stayed up at night and just pulled my hair and wanted to run away. I'm at home with the baby most of the time now.*

Julie, 16 - Sonja, 7 months

It's all right if sometimes your baby makes you feel angry and frustrated. It's all right that some mothers sometimes want to run away from home.

All mothers (and fathers) need to learn ways of dealing with this stress. Sometimes it means someone else giving you a break. It may mean leaving the housework and going to visit a friend for a change of pace. Sometimes it may mean calling a hotline. Every mother is going to have these feelings at least occasionally.

Teen moms are often reluctant to ask their fathers to babysit, but sometimes a grandfather is a fine person to watch the baby. It gives him a feeling of participating and helping his daughter through a difficult time. It gives him a way to involve himself.

## Take a Few Minutes Off

*There are times when I just want to spank her butt so hard. What I've done a few times is lay Sonja down and take a walk. There have been a couple of times at 2 a.m. when I couldn't do anything with her, so I'd lay her down and walk around the block — even though it's not the safest neighborhood in the world.*

Julie

If you start feeling tense and uptight, and you have no one else to take care of the baby, what can you do? Sometimes it's better to put her in her crib where you know she's safe, then walk away from her for a short time. This may be better for baby than if you try to cope with more than you can handle right now.

Don't feel guilty about it. Sometimes mothers do that. They know they have to get away, but they still feel guilty. It's okay. It may be necessary occasionally, especially for a single parent who can't poke a father in the back and say, "It's your turn."

Of course you should never leave your baby alone in an empty house. Julie, who mentioned walking around the block in the middle of the night, lived with her parents. Because they were home, she could leave occasionally when she was upset.

A mother living alone might ask her next-door neighbor to stay with her baby for a short time when she needs to get

away. If you need to get out for awhile, find a way to do so.
Some moms find that exercising helps them relieve
tension. You can go back to doing prenatal exercises and
other relaxation techniques you learned during pregnancy
without hurting yourself or your stitches. More vigorous
exercising should be delayed until all bleeding has stopped.
If you feel lightheaded, you should stop and rest awhile.

## What About *Your* Parents?

> *Coming home felt good. At the hospital I didn't*
> *have my mom to help me and I didn't know what to*
> *do. We'd been living at Del's house, but we came here*
> *to my mom from the hospital. She helped me a lot.*
>
> Ynez

When your baby is born, your parents may still have a
little trouble adjusting to this unplanned-for grandchild. Or
they may be thrilled with this new little person. They might
even be ready to take charge.

You'll need help those first weeks, but it's probably
better for you (and your partner if he's there) to take as
much responsibility as possible for your baby. This is the
best way for you and your baby to bond together. If you are
responsible during these early weeks, your parents are more
likely to understand that you're the parent, a hard concept
for some grandparents to accept.

As you acknowledge the stress you may be feeling at
this time, you might want to remember that your parents,
too, may be feeling quite stressed.

Will they be financially responsible for awhile for you
and baby? How will your baby's presence affect any other
children in the family?

If you're living with your family, there are a lot of
people's feelings to consider. If you've talked about this

before your baby is born, all of you will probably handle things a little better.

## Your Partner Relationship

Many young women, and many young men, too, wonder what sex will be like after their baby is born. Some moms are not in a relationship that includes sexual intercourse, but others are. Guys sometimes wonder how long you have to wait, while moms are more worried about whether it will hurt, or if they even want to do it. Actually, you may be so tired those first weeks after delivery that sex doesn't even sound interesting.

*Sex was hard for me for two months or so. We tried, but it hurt so we stopped.*

Ynez

It's important that you have a check-up before you begin to have intercourse after childbirth. The first time or two the tissue may still be tender, and each partner needs to be patient with the other. The vaginal opening will be about the same size it was before you ever had sex. At first, hormonal juices that help keep the area moist may not be working too well. Therefore, a lubricant such as KY jelly or the jellies sold for contraceptive purposes will help.

At any rate, this is a topic you and your partner should talk about *before* your baby is born. That way both of you will understand what to expect.

The two of you can also be making a decision about the kind of family planning you'll use. Remember that you could begin to ovulate as soon as two weeks after you deliver — which means you could get pregnant again. You'd probably rather concentrate on your baby now rather than starting another one right away.

*See Chapter 14 for information about family planning.*

*Breastfeeding — a beautiful experience for mother and baby.*

# 11

# Feeding
# Your Newborn

*I wanted to give her the best start.
I didn't have a house or a back
yard for her to play in, but I could
breastfeed her. She deserved the
best start she could have.*

Zandra, 16 - Dakota, 11 months

*I feel bonded to Jenilee. I think it's
because I breastfeed her. When
she cries, I'm the one that gets
her, and I feed her and she's
better. She stares up at me like she
already loves me.*

Lacey, 16 - Jenilee, 1 month

*It's so easy. We didn't have to drag
bottles and formula along when
we went camping.*

Alison, 18 - Stevie, 2 months

## Many Choose Breastfeeding

More and more young mothers are choosing to breast-feed their babies. Perhaps they've been told it's best for the baby. They feel they "owe" their baby the best care possible. For them, this includes breastfeeding.

It's also perfectly all right to choose this method because it's easier for the mom. Having no bottles to sterilize, no formula to mix, and no heating required can make life much simpler for a tired new mother. And, of course, breastfeeding is cheaper. That's good news for the pocketbook, too.

> *It's really handy. When I go places, I pump because I almost always use breast milk. I tried formula once, but Patty spit it up. I'm breastfeeding because they say it's good for the baby. But it's also handy and saves money. You don't have to get up and heat the bottle. That's when I especially like it.*
>
> Beth, 18 - Patty, 3 weeks

> *I didn't give Karl any formula for at least a month. He was completely breastfed. I stopped because I was going to work. Mostly I liked breastfeeding. I felt I was doing a little more for him, that I was giving him something directly from me.*
>
> Kimberly, 17 - Karl, 23 months

The breasts don't contain real milk for two or three days after delivery. Instead, they produce "colostrum." This is a yellowish substance which contains water, some sugar, minerals, and many important antibodies. This gives the baby some protection against illness. Even a few days of breastfeeding will give your newborn a good start.

Someone may suggest to you that breastfeeding your baby will make your breasts sag. Not so! Your breasts become larger during pregnancy, but wearing a good support bra during pregnancy and while you're breastfeeding helps prevent sagging.

Dad doesn't need to feel left out when you're breast-feeding. Help him understand that you're breast-feeding so your baby will have the best possible start. Dad can help bathe baby, change his diaper, and play with him. Babies need lots of love and cuddling when they're not eating, too.

## Less Illness for Breastfed Babies

*I know how much easier breastfeeding is for me compared to my mom's friend. She had a baby about the same time I had Stevie, and she's bottle-feeding him. He's had three colds already, and Stevie's had none. Her baby cries a lot, too.*

Alison

Another very important reason to choose breastfeeding is the fact that breastfed babies tend to be ill less often during their first year of life than are bottle-fed babies. A breastfed baby is less likely to catch a cold, for example. Have you ever cared for a tiny baby who couldn't breathe because he couldn't blow his nose? If so, you know how hard it is for both mother and baby.

Of course, breastfeeding your baby doesn't guarantee no colds for a year. And if you bottle-feed, you aren't guaranteed a certain number of colds! All we know is that breastfed babies are *less likely* to get sick than are their bottle-fed friends. They are less likely to develop allergies, ear aches, diarrhea or constipation, and tooth decay. Breastfeeding also helps your baby's brain grow.

With these facts in mind, make your own decision. If you prefer to bottle-feed your baby, fine. Above all, don't feel guilty. You certainly can be a "good" mother, no matter which feeding method you choose.

If, while you're pregnant, all of this seems confusing, perhaps you simply will decide not to decide. If you breastfeed baby for just a few days, he'll get the colostrum. If you then decide you don't like breastfeeding, switch to bottles with a clear conscience.

> *I never said, "I'm going to breastfeed." I said I'd try it for a couple of days, maybe a week, and then I'd quit if I didn't like it. I continued for 11 months!*
>
> *When I went to school my mom would give Leah formula in the morning, and then I'd breastfeed her when I got home.*

Lyra, 18 - Leah, 14 months

The exception to breastfeeding being best for baby is when Mom smokes and/or takes drugs. Drugs and nicotine are carried through the milk to the baby. Even if the drugs you're taking are prescribed, check with your healthcare provider to be sure baby would thrive on your breast milk.

Avoid over-the-counter medications when you're breastfeeding.

## Getting Started

First, let your doctor and the hospital know that you intend to breastfeed your baby. It's best to put your baby to your breast within an hour after delivery. Stress to your doctor and the hospital staff that your baby is *not* to have a bottle while he's in the hospital. Having him in your room with you is best so he can nurse whenever he wants to.

When you're ready to nurse baby, hold him on his side facing you, tummy to tummy, and touch the baby's lower lip with your finger or nipple. He'll open wide, a rooting reflex action ready to go at birth. As his mouth opens, bring him to your nipple. Check to be sure his bottom lip curls out. If it doesn't, pull down gently on his chin.

Be sure he gets as much as possible of the areola (dark area around the nipple) into his mouth as he sucks. This is where the milk pools. If he "latches on" properly, your nipples shouldn't get sore. If it hurts, break the suction, take him off, and latch him on again with more of the areola in his mouth.

When he latches on, his mouth should be about one inch behind the nipple on the areola. Latching on will hurt for less than a minute as he stretches your nipple. If it still hurts, redo the latching on.

*Latching on works because pretty much the baby takes the nipple when you rub her cheek and she turns toward you. At first I had trouble doing the football hold, and sometimes that was easier because it keeps your breast out of her face so she can breathe. You just keep trying.*

*Don't give up. And make sure, if you take her off, you break the suction so the baby doesn't hurt your breast or her mouth.*

Aimee, 17 - Amelia, 8 months

Just two or three minutes on each side each time he nurses are enough the first day. Gradually increase the time. Within a week your baby will probably nurse ten to twenty minutes on each side at each feeding.

Sometimes the soreness is because the baby sucks only on the end of your nipple. This would hurt and your baby wouldn't get as much milk. To avoid this pain, make sure your baby's mouth opens wide onto the areola. Nurse often, but not for long each time.

If you offer the left breast first at one feeding, start with the right one the next time so that baby will empty each one completely. This is important so your breasts will "know" to produce more milk on both sides. Feed your baby at the first sign of hunger, such as increased activity, mouthing, or rooting. Breastfed babies need to eat 8-12 times in a 24-hour period. Waiting until she's crying is not necessary, and may give baby more difficulty with breastfeeding.

The more often you nurse your baby, the more milk your breasts will produce. Be careful not to let your nipples get too sore those first few days. If your nipples get sore, keep them dry and expose them to air. Rub a little breast milk into each nipple after you finish feeding your baby. Avoid creams and lanolin. For persistent soreness, get help.

Whether you're breastfeeding or bottle-feeding, your breasts will feel heavy and full during the first week after your baby is born. Breastfeed your baby, and your breasts will feel more comfortable in a day or two. Sometimes it helps to put a warm washcloth on your breasts and massage them before you nurse. Massaging during feeding will also help. Expressing a little milk first may soften the areola to make it easier for the baby to latch on to a very full and hard breast. You can freeze this milk for later use.

If you're still sore after he nurses, try an ice pack under your armpits — that's where the breast tissue starts. A warm shower and breast massage may also help. Green cabbage leaves give relief much as the ice does.

If milk leaks from your breasts between feedings, you can use purchased disposable or cloth pads to protect your clothes. Probably more effective are pads you can make yourself. Cut a cloth diaper into small pieces about three inches square. Sew several layers together, then put in your bra as needed. They're easily washed.

Burp your baby after he finishes nursing at each breast. Just hold him up to your shoulder and rub his back gently. He probably won't burp as much as he would if he took a bottle. Breastfed babies don't usually swallow as much air as bottle-fed babies.

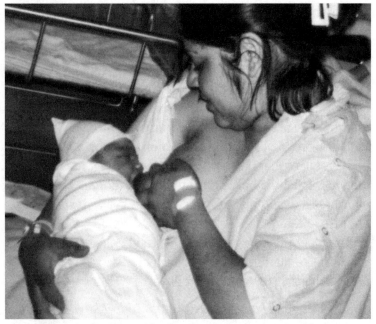

*Breastfeeding intensifies bonding between mom and baby.*

## The Art of Breastfeeding

*I had problems at first. Orlando constantly wanted to suck, and my nipples were getting sore. My mom kept telling me I was running out of milk. She couldn't breastfeed her own kids, so she seems to be totally against it.*

*I thought about trying a bottle, but Orlando is a breast baby. He loves it, and I do, too. He's already five months old, and he won't take a bottle at all. He really should so I could get out once in awhile. But within two or three months he'll be able to drink some milk from a cup.*

*He loves to breastfeed. I tried a pacifier when my nipples were sore at first, but he didn't like that. Then he started sucking his thumb, and that helped.*

Holly, 17 - Orlando, 5 months

"Orlando constantly wanted to suck, and my nipples were getting sore." True, you may have a little soreness during your first week of nursing. With good positioning and the correct latch-on, this will go away soon.

As we said above, letting your nipples air dry after feeding will help, and so will rubbing a little breast milk into the sore area after each feeding.

The more the baby sucks, the more milk one's body produces. For a good start with breastfeeding, it's best not to give the baby a bottle during the first month. This gives your breasts and your baby a chance to get well started with breastfeeding.

Some people don't realize how good colostrum is for newborns — and that newborns generally lose a few ounces the first few days after birth:

> *I tried to breastfeed Lenny but I didn't have milk for three days and he was losing weight. My mom told me to give him the bottle. Then I tried to nurse him later and he didn't want it.*
>
> Ynez, 16 - Lenny, 4 months

If Ynez had continued breastfeeding for another day or two, she might have been reassured that her breasts were making "real" milk. Giving a baby a bottle during the first week or two is likely to interfere with breastfeeding.

Remember, your breasts create more milk only if stimulated by baby's nursing — or if you express milk (squeeze out) by hand or with a breast pump.

Some experts suggest that a very young baby's daily use of a pacifier could interfere with breastfeeding. It's probably best not to give her a pacifier until breastfeeding is going well for you and your baby.

After the first few weeks, it's a good idea to give the baby a bottle occasionally so she'll know how to suck from one. There may be an emergency sometime when you can't be there. This will also give grandma and dad a chance to feed the baby.

## Is Baby Getting Enough?

If your breasts are small, don't worry. The amount of milk you make depends on how often your baby nurses. If your nipples are flat or inverted, you can wear breast shells inside your bra between feedings. These help bring out the nipples. A highly motivated baby will pull the nipples out all on his own.

If your baby doesn't seem interested in latching on to your breast at first, take off her clothes except for her diaper, and hold her close. Lots of skin to skin contact helps a baby figure out what she needs to do. Cuddle her often and try to express a little milk into her mouth. If your baby still doesn't suck, giving her a bottle is not the answer. That would only confuse her. If you need help, call a breastfeeding specialist.

Is there a La Leche League chapter in your community? La Leche League is an organization of breastfeeding mothers. A local group will usually have a series of several meetings dealing with the how-to of breastfeeding. Members are available to help each other find answers to questions or problems with breastfeeding.

Check your telephone directory. If you find the League listed, you can call to learn of meetings of possible interest to you. If you have problems with breastfeeding, you can usually get help by calling their number.

Some WIC (Supplemental Feeding Program for Women, Infants, and Children) offices have breastfeeding peer support counselors. Maternity ward nurses, lactation specialists, or possibly a breastfeeding specialist in your healthcare provider's office can also help you.

For the first month or so, you'll be feeding baby at least 8-12 times each 24 hours. You may need to wake him occasionally for feeding during the first couple of weeks. If he eats every 2-2½ hours during the day, he's likely to sleep for longer periods at night.

Is baby having at least six wet and two dirty diapers each 24 hours? Is she gaining 4-7 ounces each week? Is she content one or two hours between most feedings? And can you hear her swallow as she sucks? If so, she's getting enough to eat.

Your baby is likely to grow especially fast when she's about two weeks old, again at six weeks and three months. At these times, she needs more food. You may think you don't have enough milk for her. You're probably right.

The solution is simply to nurse baby more often. That signals your breasts to make more milk. Your baby controls your supply of milk. Usually it takes about two days of nursing more often to make more milk. Then she will level out to nursing less often again. She'll also be more content.

Breastfed babies don't need additional water or any other food for the first four to six months, according to the American Academy of Pediatrics.

## Guarding *Your* Health

Mom's good health is an important part of breastfeeding. Continue taking your prenatal vitamins. You still need the same foods you needed for a healthy pregnancy. Your weight will return to normal gradually, and even faster when you breastfeed.

If your baby seems fussy or appears to have gas, think about what you ate the day before. If you had a lot of any one food, or if you added something new, it might be affecting your baby. Cut back or eliminate that food and see if baby is happier.

*Breastfeeding in public can be managed nicely.*

## Breastfeed in Public?

*When she was little, it was harder to nurse in public, but as they grow, the baby pretty much covers you and you hardly need a blanket. It was difficult at first, but then you realize everybody thinks it's good you're breastfeeding.*

*I nurse everywhere. It may make some people uncomfortable, especially at first when I couldn't cover myself as well. At first I'd get my boyfriend or my mother or father to hold the blanket in front of me while she was latching on.*

*I plan to continue probably until she's 2. It's not like you're taking a toddler out nursing in public. It's special for them. You can do it in the morning and at night time.*

Aimee, 17 - Amelia, 8 months

Obviously breastfeeding is the natural way to feed a baby. Since babies have a habit of getting hungry no matter where they are, ideally mother and baby "should" feel comfortable nursing almost anywhere. Surely most people would agree that when baby is hungry she should be fed.

In some areas, however, breastfeeding is not often done in public places — a custom which can make life hard for a hungry baby and her mother if they don't happen to be home at mealtime.

Sometimes mothers choose to bottle-feed because they think they would have to stay home to breastfeed the baby. Many mothers, however, feel comfortable throwing a blanket completely over the baby while she nurses. Usually, people assume she's asleep.

## Some Prefer Bottle-Feeding

*I decided on bottle-feeding mostly because of the time — and because my mother bottle-fed all of her babies. I tried breastfeeding in the hospital, and I didn't like it. Sterilizing the bottles doesn't take much time. I use pre-mixed formula — no mixing to do.*

Vicki, 17 - Deanna, 3 weeks

*Always hold baby while you feed her, whether with breast or bottle.*

*I breastfed Dennis the first two months, and I'm glad I did. I think it was worth it because it was more convenient then. I also felt closer to him. That's probably why he slept so much and was such a good baby. But I changed to formula recently mostly for my own convenience. With summer here, I wanted a little more freedom. I also wanted Ted to be able to feed him.*

Andrea, 17 - Dennis, 3 months

Lots of babies do fine on carefully prepared formula. To make formula, simply follow the directions found in every package/can of prepared formula. Boil the water you use in the formula, or use bottled water. If baby is lovingly held while he drinks his bottle, he probably feels about as good emotionally as he would if he were breastfed.

Of course you'll *never* lay baby down with a propped bottle. The love and cuddling he gets from you during his mealtimes is extremely important, whether you breast- or bottle-feed him. Check the size of the nipple holes occasionally. They should be just big enough so the formula drips slowly from the bottle when you hold it upside down. If the formula comes out too fast, the holes are too big. He won't get enough sucking as he drinks. The only solution is to buy new nipples.

Whether you breastfeed or feed your baby with a bottle, eating time can be a period of special closeness for the two of you. Talk to her as she eats. Tell her how much you love her. Let her know how much you like this part of your day, and she will respond more and more as the days go by.

A baby being held and fed by a loving, unhurried parent is learning that most important lesson — to trust her world and you. *Cherish the time you have together.*

*For more information, see **Why Should I Nurse My Baby?** by Pamela Wiggins (*Noodle Soup).

**Face - may have some soft hair**

**Eyes - slightly puffy**

**Nose - small, flat bridge**

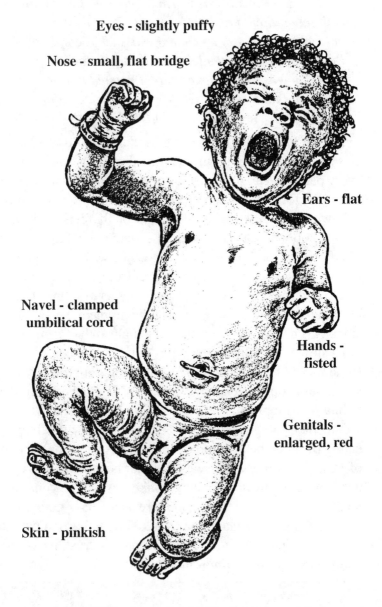

**Ears - flat**

**Navel - clamped
umbilical cord**

**Hands -
fisted**

**Genitals -
enlarged, red**

**Skin - pinkish**

*Your baby is likely to be born with the above characteristics.*

# 12

# What Does a New Baby Do?

*When I first saw Patty, I thought, "Golly, was that inside me for nine months?" She didn't look very pretty — too white and awfully tiny. But the doctor said her color would come soon, and it did.*

Beth, 18 - Patty, 3 weeks

*When Racquelle came out, I said, "She's all purple!" Her head was shaped a little funny because they used forceps. She was all messy. They held her up and let me kiss her. I almost started crying — you get a real good feeling.*

Cheryl, 15 - Racquelle, 2 months

## What Does She Look Like?

Labor is called labor because it's such hard work for the
mother. But it's also hard on baby. A just-born baby
doesn't look at all like the charming little person in the
diaper commercials. Instead, she may seem forlorn and
look a bit stressed.

Nearly every mother, father, and grandparent, however,
will swear she is the most beautiful baby ever born!

> *It was instant love . . . but still it was hard to*
> *believe Dennis was here, that what was inside of me*
> *was now a little baby. I thought he was cute. What I*
> *liked best was his little neck — he didn't have any!*
>
> Andrea, 17 - Dennis, 3 months

Most babies look pretty messy after delivery until the
nurse cleans them up. Often a baby's head becomes molded
during labor and delivery. Instead of looking round like
most people's heads, hers seems longer than it should.
Sometimes there are bumps and lumps on her head, too.

> *At first I thought Dennis was ugly. He had a big*
> *lump on his head right in front, but it was down the*
> *next day.*
>
> Ted, 19, Dennis' father

At birth, the bones in baby's head are soft enough to
change shape slightly in order to go through the birth canal.
Within a few days baby's head will become round. If her
mother is in labor a long time, baby's head is more likely to
undergo molding.

Regardless of their ethnic origin, most babies are fairly
red when they're born, sometimes even purplish looking.
By the time she goes home from the hospital, her skin will
look better. When she cries, her skin may turn red and
blotchy. This, too, is normal.

Black babies' skin is often lighter at birth than it will be later. The skin at the tip of the ear is a good indication of the baby's permanent color.

Babies have a "soft spot" (fontanelle), actually more than one, on the top of their heads. Some people are afraid of the soft spot. They think baby might be injured if the soft spot is touched. However, this spot is covered with a tough membrane which gives plenty of protection.

The skull doesn't close over the soft spot for about 18 months. During that time, it's important to wash the baby's head thoroughly to prevent cradle cap. Cradle cap is a scaliness similar to heavy dandruff which sometimes develops on a baby's head. When you give your baby a shampoo, just massage her head with your finger tips as you would your own. Touching the soft spot is not going to hurt it.

If cradle cap does develop, the best way to treat it is to wash baby's head with a low-allergy soap or clean her head with a soft brush. You can also use baby oil. Apply it with cotton or a soft brush, then wash it off in a few minutes.

## Belly Button Care

*Today Evan's belly button cord fell off. I went to change him and I found it stuck to his diaper. I'm glad it came off because I thought it was ugly.*

Brandy, 15 - Evan, 1 week

Newborn babies have a couple of inches of umbilical cord still attached to their navels. This cord turns black and usually drops off within a week. Most doctors suggest that baby not be put in water until after the cord drops off. Sometimes the area bleeds a little those first few days. It can be cleaned gently with cotton dipped in alcohol.

Some babies' belly buttons stick out more than usual. In

the past, people often put snug binders on their babies —
pieces of cloth wrapped firmly around the baby's middle.
Sometimes people put tape over the navel or even taped a
penny or other flat item over it. They thought this would
keep it from sticking out. Actually, it won't help, and it can
cause irritation.

*Kamie and I lived with Lucas and his mom for four
months. His mom would tell me to do things that
didn't sound right. For example, she told me to put a
handkerchief around Kamie's belly button, and fasten
it real tight. I felt like it was giving her a stomach-
ache plus I was afraid the safety pin would open. His
mom kept saying Kamie's belly button would look ugly
if I didn't do that. Finally I got mad and I took it off.*
                                    Kelsey, 19 - Kamie, 21 months

If baby's belly button sticks out, it sticks out. That's all
right. This condition usually disappears sometime during
childhood. If it sticks out a lot, however, ask your doctor to
check for umbilical hernia.

---

**Umbilical hernia:** A bulge near the belly button
where the abdominal muscles come together.

---

## How Baby Develops

If you know something about your baby's development,
you'll find him more interesting. And if you think he's
interesting, you'll give him more attention. If you give him
more attention, he'll respond more to you. A beautiful
circle to enter!

Of course all babies are different. Even at birth, your
baby will look different than other babies in the hospital
nursery. He may cry a lot, or he may be quiet much of the
time. Most babies sleep a great deal the first weeks, but

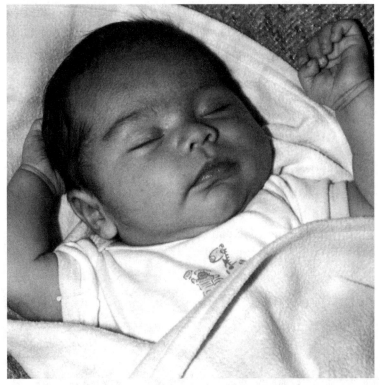

*Most newborns sleep a lot those first few days.*

yours may stay awake several hours a day. Accept him as he is and love him.

A newborn human is far more helpless than is a new kitten, colt, or other baby animal. He depends completely on his parents or other caregivers for survival.

When you put your newborn to bed, lay her on her back. To prevent SIDS (Sudden Infant Death Syndrome), most experts recommend that a baby sleep on her back.

Babies usually respond to sounds at birth. She will startle at a loud noise, perhaps cry.

She can hear rather well. Of course she doesn't understand your words, but she likes the sound of your loving voice. After all, during the last few months before birth, she

was "hearing" your voice, or at least feeling the rhythm of
it, while she was in your uterus. Now it's important to talk
and sing to her. Loud sharp noises and angry voices will
upset her, but she loves your gentle voice.

*When I change Sonja's diaper, I always talk to her
and play with her. I talk to her when I feed her, too.
She always likes that.*

Julie, 16 - Sonja, 7 months

## What Can He See?

He can't see well when he's born. The world probably
looks hazy to him. He can see objects best which are about

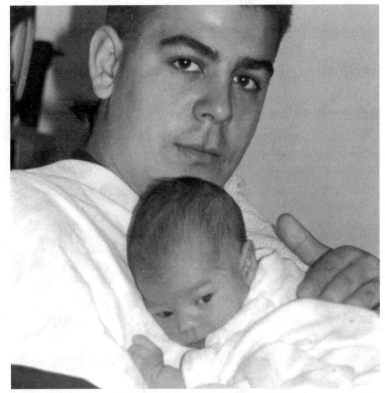

*He doesn't see very well yet.*

nine inches from his eyes. When he's breastfeeding, this is about the distance between his and his mother's eyes.

Sometimes parents worry about their newborn's eyes. They seem hazy, and sometimes even appear to be crossed. The baby can't focus well yet because nerve connections between her brain and eye muscles aren't complete. Her vision and control will develop gradually, and soon her eyes will stay put.

At birth, most babies' eyes are dark blue or gray. Their eyes will gradually change to their permanent coloring. Some dark-skinned infants are born with dark brown eyes.

Sometime between birth and six weeks of age, most babies can begin to follow an object for a short distance with their eyes. You can easily "test" this ability with your baby.

### Test Baby's Vision

Use a big object with strong contrasting tones. A piece of cardboard that is at least five inches across and has black and white squares on it works well. Choose a time when your baby is awake and comfortable. Hold the cardboard about twelve inches from his eyes. Move it slowly from one side to the other. Do his eyes follow? For how long?

At first, he may show interest for only a few seconds. By the time he is two or three months old, he may watch the item as it moves all the way from one side of his head to the other.

Her favorite "object" is your face. She may look at you occasionally almost from birth. Sometime between birth and about two months of age, she will smile at you. It's an exciting milestone.

In the past, experts insisted that if a new baby looked

like she was smiling, it was not a real smile. True, her smile
may be partly a reflex, but it usually happens when she is
content. An awake baby begins to smile in response to
someone at around one month.

> **Suggestion:** Since your newborn is most interested
> in looking at faces, make her a "face" for her crib. The
> simplest way is to draw colorful features on a paper
> plate. Attach the plate to the side of the crib about ten
> inches from her head. Choose the side of the crib
> toward which she most often looks.

A non-glass crib mirror or a picture of you would be fun
for baby, too. Before long, she will enjoy looking at her
reflection.

In most states, newborns receive a hearing test before
they leave the hospital. A few babies will need retesting. If
you're told your baby needs this retesting, be sure you get
it done.

## Notice Her Reflex Actions

Baby's behavior at birth is mostly reflex action.

> **Reflex action:** Responding to something
> without having to learn to do so.

Rooting and sucking are reflex actions. While a newborn
usually needs some help in finding the nipple, he generally
knows how to suck once he gets there.

A new baby is not quiet, even when he's not crying. He
will hiccup, startle, and shake because his nervous system
is still immature. This is not a problem. Sometimes, however, a young mother needs reassurance:

*Once I got scared because Nick started shaking*

*and making weird sounds after I fed him. It was one
a.m., and I woke Paul up. He said Nick had the
hiccups, so I relaxed.*

Theresa, 16 - Nick, 6 months

Another reflex action exhibited by a newborn baby is the
"walking" reflex. If you hold him upright with his feet just
touching a firm surface, he will take "steps." He will
actually place one foot after another while you support his
weight.

This lasts only a week or so. Then if you hold him
upright, he will simply sag rather than making walking
movements.

Baby's hands are almost always clenched into fists
during the first month or two. This, too, is a reflex action. If
you put your finger in his fist and pull back gently, you'll
find surprising strength in that little fist.

## Those First Days

*He was awake a lot at night, every three or four
hours, but I enjoyed being with him, I really did. He'd
sleep a lot, then he'd wake up just to eat, then he'd go
right back to sleep. And I was thinking that whoever
he spends the most time with he will think is his mom.
So I thought, even when I'd get frustrated, I have to
spend every minute with him.*

Camelia, 16 - Buchanan, 6 months

The main thing you may notice about your newborn is
her sleepiness. During her first days of life "outside," she
will probably be alert only about three minutes per hour on
the average. She will be even less alert at night (you hope).
This "alert" time is in addition to the time baby spends
crying because she is hungry, wet, generally uncomfortable, or lonely, and the time she spends eating.

All babies lose a few ounces during the first two or three days after birth. This is perfectly normal. Baby will gain it all back within a few days.

Babies, both boys and girls, sometimes have swollen breasts for a few days after delivery. This is caused by the hormones in the mother's body. Sometimes the baby's breast will contain a little milk. This is called witch's milk in some cultures. This is normal and will go away within a few days.

Girl babies sometimes have a slight amount of bleeding

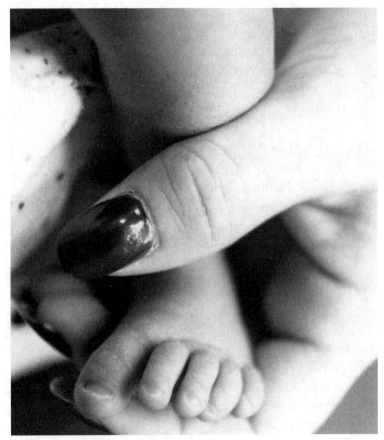

*Such a tiny foot . . .*

from the vagina for two or three days after delivery. This, too, is caused by mother's hormones. It's nothing to worry about.

Newborn boys often have very large testicles. In fact, both boys and girls have oversized genitals which appear swollen and red at birth. These are also caused by the mother's hormones. They will become smaller within a couple of weeks.

A boy baby may get an erect penis when you change him. This normally occurs occasionally throughout infancy and early childhood. It's not a problem. Neither is it a problem if your girl or boy baby touches her/his genitals. It's absolutely normal.

Baby may have birthmarks. Some of these will disappear in time. "Strawberry" marks and dark moles, however, generally stay on baby for life. These marks tend to run in families, and you can do nothing to make them go away.

Dark-colored marks may also be on African American or Hispanic babies. Most often they are on or above the buttocks. These marks usually fade by the time the child is two years old.

Newborns may develop or are born with baby acne. Caused by hormonal imbalance, these are little white heads that will disappear in a couple of weeks. No treatment is needed.

## Observe Him Closely

If the baby becomes too warm, she may develop miliaria (prickly heat). These are little white heads on the surface of the skin, usually on the nose and cheeks. To prevent them, don't overdress your baby. Babies need about the same amount of clothing that you need. This does *not* mean wrapping her in a warm blanket on a hot summer day!

Thirty to fifty percent of all full-term and eighty percent

of premature babies develop jaundice which causes their skin or the whites of their eyes to get yellowish. There are several causes, most of which have to do with the baby's immaturity.

Should your baby look yellowish, check with the doctor. Extra blood tests will be given, and the treatment could be as simple as giving her water to drink. Occasionally, special lights may be used to get rid of the yellow skin color.

The best treatment for jaundice that first week is to breastfeed often, at least every 11/2-2 hours. Put your baby near a window to sleep during the day because daylight helps the baby get rid of jaundice. If the room is warm enough, dress baby only in a diaper so the light can get to his skin.

Baby's bowel movements are worth watching. New babies have greenish BMs that are softer than those of an adult. If color, texture, and odor are normal, the number doesn't matter much.

A breastfed baby will usually have a yellowish BM every time she nurses. That's because a breastfed baby digests the milk faster than does a bottle-fed baby. This is good for her.

The first bowel movement a baby has after birth is called meconium. Meconium is a greenish-black sticky substance which fills the intestines of babies before they are born. Almost all babies pass meconium during the first day, sometimes for three or four days. Ted, a young father, commented, "Those black poops freaked me out!"

## What Does Baby Want Out of Life?

*That first month was not what I expected. I thought taking care of Chandra would be easy, but it was hard. When she cried I thought I could just pick her up and she'd go to sleep right away. But she didn't.*

*It was more work than I expected. I had to fix her
formula, change her diapers — I didn't think she'd be
wet all the time. She had to be changed constantly. I'd
be watching TV, and I'd hear her crying. I'd get kind
of mad because I didn't want to move.*

Maria, 18 - Chandra, 6 weeks

Your newborn is a very sensitive little creature. She will
probably startle and cry at any sudden change. If there is a
loud noise or if her bassinet is jolted, she may cry. If you
lift her suddenly from her bed, she may cry.

When you pick her up she will feel more secure if you
put your hands carefully under her, then wait a second or
two before you lift her. She'll then have time to adjust to
being moved.

Of course you *always* provide head support for a young
baby when you lift or hold her.

Comfort is the most important thing to a newborn.
Comfort first of all means having her needs met. Letting
her "cry it out" makes sense only when you can't do anything to help her feel better. Even then, most babies prefer
to be held in their misery.

Nearly every baby loves to be touched, held, and
cuddled. They have a way of snuggling into your arms that
makes both you and baby feel good. When baby is fussy,
holding her upright with her head near your shoulder may
quiet her.

## Infants Don't "Spoil"

*I talked to my great-grandmother before she died
(before I was pregnant), and she said, "I never let any
of my babies cry. Whenever a baby cries, it has a
need, even if it's just to be held." So that was stuck in
my head.*

*Your loving care is an important part of her brain development.*

*So when Sonja was little, if she cried, I fed her. If she cried and wanted to be picked up, I picked her up. My mom would tell me I would spoil her. She was eating every two hours until she was about 2 1/2 months old.*

Julie

Most parents, if they let themselves go, love holding their baby. Touch her, love her. Above all, don't worry about spoiling her in these early months.

Babies are born with 100 billion brain cells just waiting to develop. They develop because of stimulation, like lights and sound (especially the sound of their parents' voices). Touch is so important that babies who are rarely touched or played with have smaller brains! The greatest amount of brain activity is between birth and three years.

Young parents often ask, "If I pick her up when she

cries, won't she think she can get whatever she wants by crying?" This old idea simply isn't true.

Yes, she'll cry when she needs something, and she will learn something from the parent who answers her cries. She'll learn a basic sense of trust in her world. And that sense of trust is the most important thing she can learn during her first months.

By the way, research shows that babies who are picked up often during their first months cry *less* at one year of age than do the children who weren't picked up when, as infants, they cried.

So hold your baby. Pick her up when she cries. Feed her if she's hungry. (See chapter 11, "Feeding Your Newborn.") Change her if she's wet or messy. Keep her clean, dry, warm (but not too warm), and fed.

## Perhaps She's Lonely

*When Chandra gets uncomfortable, she just cries and cries and I don't know what to do. My mom works so she's not here during the day to advise me.*

Maria

If she's not hungry, perhaps she's uncomfortable for some other reason. Does she need changing? Was she burped enough at her last feeding? Is she perhaps too warm? Or is she too cold?

If nothing seems to work, perhaps she's lonely. Have you ever thought about what it must be like to be able to do nothing except lie in a bassinet by yourself? For nine months, you've been carried securely in your mother's uterus, then suddenly you're outside. And you're expected to sleep by yourself with no human contact. That's quite a change for your baby!

Perhaps she simply wants to be held. Do you have a

rocking chair? Use it! A rocking cradle is also nice for a
baby. Sing to her as you rock her.

> *Babies like to be held close. Our friend, when her
> baby cries, sets him out on her knees and bounces him
> up and down. He just cries harder because he doesn't
> like it. Poor little baby, I feel so sorry for him.*
>
> *When Stevie cries, we pick him up and hold him
> close and love him. I think that's pretty important
> instead of sticking him out there on your knees.*
>
> *I love rocking Stevie. The one thing my mother
> insisted on buying before he was born was that
> rocking chair, and now I know why.*
>
> Alison, 18 - Stevie, 2 months

If money for baby things is limited, your baby would
undoubtedly rather you'd buy a cheap unpainted or used
crib *and* a rocking chair, rather than just a fancy crib.

## He May Like Swaddling

Sometimes swaddling helps a fussy baby. This practice
of wrapping baby tightly in a blanket is common in many
cultures. After being somewhat cramped before birth, baby
may feel more secure if she is wrapped snugly.

To swaddle a baby, center her on the blanket with her
head just over one edge. Pick up an upper corner of the
blanket and bring it down diagonally over her shoulder. Her
elbow will be inside, but one hand should be free. Tuck the
corner under baby's knees.

Pull up the other side of the blanket and fold it snugly
over baby. Lift her a little so you can put the edge of the
blanket under her.

You'll have a snugly wrapped baby, and you may have a
more contented baby. In fact, some infants will sleep better
if they're swaddled as they're put to bed.

## Be Sensitive to Her Needs

*When Stevie is asleep, we let him sleep. A lot of
people don't realize this. I've seen friends wake their
babies up just because they have company. I think it's
important to pick him up when he cries. Or if he's
awake and not crying and you want to pick him up,
fine. But not when he's sleeping. It's just as important
to let him sleep as it is to pick him up when he cries.*

Alison

Your newborn infant is a very interesting person who
knows more than we used to think. This is when you begin
to be a big influence on your child's behavior. The kind of
home you have and the things you do are important to
your baby.

You have an exciting challenge as you care for her, teach
her, and love her.

*For more information, see **Your Baby and Child from Birth to
Age Five** by Penelope Leach (Knopf).*

*Fulfilling your role as father is very special.*

# 13

# Especially for Dad

*I was with Hillary when we learned she was pregnant. It was the biggest change in my life I could ever imagine. We went in to have a physical, everything was normal, like an average day.*

*We come out, and it's like everything from that point on has changed.*

*I can't consider myself a teenager any more because I'm a parent.*

*I think my daughter is going to always come first. I'm going to try to meet her needs before I meet mine.*

Brady, 17 - Bronwyn, 10 months

*I'm going to do for Blair what I didn't get. My
father wasn't always doing right. He wasn't around
much. I took that into account, and I'm going to be a
better father than I had.*

*We broke up for awhile, and people would say,
"But what about the baby?" I was leaving Brooke,
not the baby. I'm not going to give up and walk out
because Brooke has an attitude.*

*If we should really break up, I would continue to
have a relationship with my son.*

Joel, 19 - Blair, 3 months

## For Teen Fathers

If you're a teen father, or you're going to be one soon,
what about you? As you probably know, many people think
teen fathers don't care about their babies or their babies'
mothers. They think teen fathers only want to make as
many girls pregnant as possible, then forget about their
responsibilities to those young women and the children
they bear.

Of course many teen fathers aren't like that at all. You
probably aren't or you wouldn't be reading this book.

You may be living with your baby's mother. You may
be married, although only one in six teenage mothers is
married to the father of her baby at the time of birth.

Perhaps you aren't living together but you spend a great
deal of time at her house, and you expect to spend more
after your baby is born. You may not have planned to be a
father so soon, but you plan to parent this child together.

*It was on Thanksgiving Day. She phoned me and
told me. At first I figured, "Maybe she just thinks she
is. How could I get somebody pregnant?" Then I got
to thinking. Was it mine or somebody else's? You*

*know, all that.*

*I used to go around doing whatever I wanted to do. Then I started realizing she was pregnant with my kid, and I started caring more and more. When she started showing, I felt there was a little of me in there along with a little of her. That's a good feeling.*

*My friends would say, "You're going to be a father?" They was cool about it. One of my buddies said, "Man, you ain't going to have no money. Everything you make is going for this kid." But everybody else wanted to be the godfather.*

*I'm supposed to graduate in four months, and I want to go in the Air Force. We'll get married after she graduates two years from now.*

*I want to be all the way involved with my baby. My kid is going to come first before anybody.*

Norm, 17 - LaTisha, 9 months pregnant

## If You're Older

If you're not a teenager, but your baby's mother is still in her teens, you'll find most of this chapter applies to you, too.

If one partner is several years older than the other one, their interests may be quite different. Parenting together in spite of those differences will take extra caring and understanding from each of you.

*Our biggest problem is that Mitzuko finds fun in going to football games and to high school dances, and I already did those things. I go to them now and they're just dumb. Like the prom. We had a real big misunderstanding about the prom. I'll be almost 22 when she has her prom, and I don't feel like going there. All those people are so young.*

Maurice, 21 - Lana, 14 months

Maurice may decide to go to the prom simply to please Mitzuko. In turn, Mitzuko may be willing to go out with Maurice's friends occasionally, friends she may not find terribly exciting.

If your partner is much younger, or you feel she's less mature, it may be tempting to play the father role with her. Both you and your baby will be better off, however, if you and your partner respect each other as equals, and each of you takes a major role in parenting your child.

Just because you are no longer a teenager doesn't mean you're completely relaxed about parenting your child. In addition to the emotional support even very young fathers can provide, you, if you're over 18, are financially responsible right now. You may still be in school, and supporting your baby may be quite difficult.

As your relationship with your child grows, however, you will probably find parenting to be one of the most rewarding jobs you will ever have.

## If You Aren't Together

You and your baby's mother may not be together. Perhaps you split up even before she knew she was pregnant, but you still want to see your baby. You're still his father whatever your relationship with his mother. Miguel was in this situation:

*I had just gotten out of jail when Maurine got pregnant. I wanted to straighten up, but I really didn't have feelings for anybody. I wanted to mess around.*

*I didn't know for two months, and we weren't together then. When I found out, I thought, "I've got to do something. This is my first child, and I'm not going to abandon him." I didn't want my child to grow up not knowing me.*

*Finally we got back together about a month before
Genny was born. Before that, I felt like I did
something wrong. I felt guilty, because if I had known
Maurine was pregnant I wouldn't have messed around
with anybody else. I would have stayed with Maurine.
I wasn't mad at her.*

*I went with Maurine to the hospital, and that's the
best thing you can ever see, your child being born. We
didn't live together, but I started keeping Genny on
weekends. I was working, and I would take care of
her. I liked that. I had never done anything like
that before.*

*Maurine and Genny started living with me a couple
of months later, and I'd get up with Genny at least
half the time.*

*We lived together for nearly a year, but then they
moved back with Maurine's folks. I still see a lot of
Genny, and I'd like to live with them again.*

Miguel, 19 - Genny, 18 months

## Father's Rights

If Maurine should decide she doesn't want Miguel to see
Genny, what are his rights?

If the baby's father is providing some financial support
— and usually even if he's not — he has a right to see his
baby. Legally, he may be able to have his child with him
part of the time. If the young parents disagree on this
matter, they should talk to a lawyer or legal aid group.

If your partner doesn't want you to see your baby,
perhaps you can do something about it. First, have you
declared paternity?

If you and your baby's mother are not married, it's
important that you establish paternity. This means that
you both sign legal papers stating you are the father of

your child. If you don't, your child might not be able to claim Social Security, insurance benefits, veterans' and other types of benefits through you. This is also the only legal way for an unmarried father to establish his right to visitation or custody.

Fathers have a right to see their child, and sometimes they need to take the initiative. It's a good idea to keep a record of your visits with your child, and to get written receipts for the money you provide for child support. This information could help if you ever need to prove in court your interest in your child.

Esteban and Trudy were both 15 when they realized Trudy was pregnant. At first, Esteban tried to avoid the issue of his approaching fatherhood. At the same time, he didn't want to desert his child as his father had deserted him and his mother:

*It was a shock to me. I didn't want to be a father. I was too young. I thought we were just playing around, and all at once Trudy came up with something real serious. She lived around the block from me, and I tried to avoid her.*

*I ran away from it for awhile, but then I went back to her. My dad left when I was born, and I didn't want that for my baby.*

*I went out with other girls all though her pregnancy. I figured after the baby was born I'd have to settle down with this one chick, so I wanted to date while I could.*

*Trudy was moody, always snapping. She was scared too, but she didn't pressure me. I kept telling her I wasn't going to leave her, but I never told her why I was never home when she called.*

*I wasn't with her in the hospital because her dad*

*don't like me. I didn't see Nathan until he was
a week old.*

*I used to gang bang a lot while she was pregnant,
but after he was born I changed. When I saw my kid,
how he looked just like me, I calmed down.*

*I dropped out of school because we didn't have any
money. I got a job, but then I started back to school
last fall. Next month I'm going back on independent
study because we need more money. I have to go back
to work.*

Esteban, 18 - Nathan, 2; Ralph, 5 months

## Her Parents May Reject You

Even if you have a job, your partner's parents may not
want you around. The parents of many teenage mothers
have little use for their grandchild's father. They blame him
for their daughter's too-quick shift from being a carefree
teenager to a hard-working mother.

*We were pretty close, her parents and I. Then when
they found out she was pregnant, they had anger for
me. I wasn't wanted in their house. Now, after the
baby was born, they seem pretty happy, and they like
me again.*

*It really puts you down when they reject you, and
that's what they were doing. But I stuck in there
because in my heart I wanted to be with my son or
daughter. I used to say to Darlene, "I understand why
they feel like that, but why don't they give us a
chance?"*

Manuel, 18 - Juan, 27 months; Darcy, 13 months

Pregnant teenagers tend to grow up fast. The physical
changes they're experiencing seem to help them realize
they are indeed facing great changes in their lives. If a

partner is not closely involved, it's hard for him to understand.

If he is involved, he may still find it difficult to cope with her moodiness. She may not be as much fun to be with as she was before she became pregnant. As her pregnancy progresses, she may focus more and more on her baby.

*We were real close, and Don was happy I was pregnant. He'd always say stuff like he was going to spoil me and the baby, he couldn't wait, etc. He'd call to see how I was.*

*We broke up when I was four months pregnant because I'd never go out with him. Don said I was grouchy and no fun any more.*

Liz, pregnant at 15

Most parents would probably have a hard time feeling positive toward this young man. He's responsible for their daughter's pregnancy, yet he complains because she's "no fun any more." In fact, Liz' parents are determined that neither Liz nor her baby will ever see Don again.

## *Your* Parents' Reaction

Sometimes it's the young man's family who is most upset about the pregnancy. Becoming a father too soon can damage their son's chances of reaching his career goals. This is not what they wanted for him. Some parents, although disappointed, will provide extra support for their son at this time, knowing that this is the best way to help him become independent as soon as possible.

*After Deborah got the pregnancy test, we were real scared because she was a cheerleader and she wanted to go to all the football games that year. And I didn't expect to be a father. We considered abortion. I wasn't ready for this.*

Then Deborah said she was going to have the baby with or without me. If I wasn't willing to go through with it, I could go home and forget her. That was too much guilt for me to handle.

I talked to my mom. She said Deborah could move in because she wasn't getting along with her mom. We ditched school for a few days, and my mom had a fit. She said if we did that, Deborah had to move back home. She said we both had to get jobs and go to

*Dad and baby bond together.*

*school, and we had to keep the house clean.*
*I've been working after school at a meat market*
*since that time. Deborah's working, too. She had*
*planned to go to college, but that won't be for awhile.*
Nathaniel, 18 (Deborah, 17 - 8 months pregnant)

## Your Responsibilities as a Dad

It's important that you do all you can to support your
family financially. You probably need to get a job as soon
as possible. Continuing your education, however, is also
extremely important.

If you're a teenager, you may find it difficult to "take
your responsibilities" as a father. If you haven't finished
high school, or even if you have, finding a good job isn't
easy. The unemployment rate among teenage men is high.

If you're not working, people around you may think you
don't want to be responsible for your child. If you've
dropped out of school, it's even easier for them to write you
off as a typical teen father, someone who will force his
baby's mother to rely on welfare for financial support. In
any case, with welfare reform, even that support will be
seriously limited for single mothers.

Legally, any man who fathers a child is expected to
provide at least half the money needed to care for that child
until s/he is 18. That's a scary thought for a teenager with
no job. Taking that responsibility at age 15 — or even 18
— may be impossible.

If you realize how much it costs to support a baby, you
may feel like giving up. Many young fathers do. They can't
get a good enough job to take care of their families by
themselves, so they provide little or no help. When we
consider the money part of being a father, it's no wonder so
many teenage fathers walk away.

Norm explained why he didn't do that:

*Babies are expensive, but it's like, well, instead of
me getting a pair of shoes, I'll give my baby this. I
can't see why guys, when they have kids, don't get
involved. I see the babies with their moms and I
wonder, "How can you have a kid in this world and
not want it? It's a part of you." I couldn't have my kid
running around without me being involved.*

Norm

Will you need to change your lifestyle because of your
baby? Zelia was worried about her partner's involvement in
a gang:

*I'm with the father right now but I wish I wasn't.
He's a gang member. That's what attracted me at first,
his appearance. Now that I'm pregnant, I don't want
my daughter to have anything to do with anything
like that.*

*My boyfriend wants his best friend to be my
daughter's godfather, and he's a gang member too.*

*He tells me "I'm going to take the baby to the gang
meetings."*

*I told him, "No, you're not, you aren't going to take
her anywhere."*

Zelia, 17 - 4 months pregnant

Some young men decide to leave their gang because of
their appoaching responsibilities as a father. Perhaps
they've had enough of the violence and they're ready for a
change. Or they may leave at least partly because it's
important to their partner that they do so:

*I've been with his dad almost three years. At first
Riley wasn't really my type. He was a little gang
banger, shaved head, big clothes. My first thought
was, he's a troublemaker. Once I got to be his friend I*

*realized he had a real sensitive side. Within a couple*
*of weeks he started changing. He let his hair grow*
*out, he got more fitted pants. He still hung out with his*
*friends, but it came to the point where he had to*
*choose between his friends or me, and he chose me.*

Denay, 16 - Dorian, 11 months

Becoming a parent generally means a big change in lifestyle. For some young people, those changes may require a
great deal of courage and determination. Speaking of his
former gang involvement, Riley, 18, commented:

*I hurt a lot of people, but once my son was born, I*
*just couldn't do it. Now I can't just think of myself, I have*
*my son to think of. I have a beautiful baby and he needs a*
*lot of love.*

## Don't Drop Out!

Esteban, quoted earlier, had dropped out of school when
he learned Trudy was pregnant. He returned to school, but
is planning now to drop out again because they need more
money. He feels he has to get a job.

That's a hard decision. Dropping out of school will
probably mean Esteban won't be able to get a well-paying
job. In fact, without even a high school diploma, he may
never make enough money to support his family as he'd
like. If he must go to work, he's wise at least to enroll in his
school's independent study program.

Esteban also needs to get some good career counseling.
Perhaps his school has a career center where he can learn
about job training. Some intensive job training now would
help him avoid being stuck in a job with no future.

Shaun had his high school diploma and was in college
when he learned he'd be a father soon. With help from his
parents, he's continuing his education. He figures this is the

most responsible thing he can do for his family at this time:

*I was shocked at the pregnancy test. I cried with her. For a couple of weeks you can't think. I was in college and knew I wanted to stay there. That was a priority. I'd have a baby to take care of, and I had to get through college. I hoped my parents would understand and help me, and they've been pretty wonderful.*

*I figured if I didn't stay in school, there wouldn't be many good jobs I could get. I decided I'd rather struggle the next couple of years rather than struggle for the rest of our lives.*

Shaun, 19 (Beth Ann, pregnant at 17)

A too-early pregnancy is likely to upset the parents of the teenagers involved. Shaun's parents' support meant he could continue his college education.

## Dad's Role During Pregnancy

Financial support isn't the only thing a father can contribute. When a couple is together during pregnancy, whether or not they live together, dad can play an important role in helping her have a healthy pregnancy. After all, it's his baby, too. If your girlfriend or wife is pregnant, you can encourage her to eat the foods she and your baby need.

*When she was pregnant, I used to cook for her. I'd fix her eggs in the morning, and I'd make salads for her. I never used to like cooking, but I'd say, "She's got to get some food inside that baby."*

Manuel

Statistically, teenage mothers are more likely to deliver babies who are too small and born too soon for optimal health. If the mother eats the foods she and her baby need throughout pregnancy, if she stays away from alcohol, cigarettes, and drugs, and if she sees her doctor regularly, she probably will have a healthy baby. You can help her do so.

*When Beth Ann was pregnant I'd get on her case to see that she ate right and got to the doctor. I was like a watchdog for her. I was very upset that she quit going to school. I'd like her out of school as soon as possible. Her high school diploma is very important, and I think she agrees.*

Shaun

If you and your partner go out partying, she may be tempted by the alcohol and drugs. Perhaps you'll decide to help her by being a good example yourself. If you don't drink or take drugs, it will probably be easier for her not to give these things to your unborn child.

If the mother smokes, the unborn child suffers. In chapter 5, page 76, Meghan explains how her boyfriend helped her quit smoking during her second pregnancy.

Being in a smoke-filled room is hard on a fetus. If you smoke, perhaps you'll choose to cut back, maybe quit because of your baby. If not, try not to smoke around your partner and unborn child.

## Sharing Prenatal Care Visits

Are you able to go to the doctor with her for each prenatal health checkup? She would appreciate your support. It's also part of becoming close to your child even before s/he is born. Listening to your unborn baby's heartbeat through the doctor's doptone (ultrasound stethoscope) is exciting. So is seeing the ultrasound, the "picture" the doctor may take of the fetus.

Randy and Whitney couldn't be together for several months during Whitney's pregnancy. He mentioned the ultrasound as making him feel a little more involved:

> *We both knew she was pregnant when I left, but Whitney didn't tell her parents until I came back. She was seven months then.*
>
> *We wrote to each other during that time, and she sent me a couple of ultrasounds. That made the baby more real for me.*
>
> *When Whitney was pregnant I was happy and scared at the same time. I was scared about what was going to happen, but happy about having him. I didn't walk out because we both agreed to have this baby, and I wanted to see my daughter or son. I didn't want the baby to suffer. That's why I didn't walk out on Whitney. It's pretty scary.*
>
> *When I came back, Whitney was real grouchy. She stayed with her parents until Keegan was born. Then she moved in with me and my parents.*
>
> *I graduate this year. I had planned to go to college, but now I'll have to get a job instead.*
>
> Randy, 17 - Keegan, 2 months

Your emotional support is probably the most important thing you can offer your partner right now. Whether the pregnancy is planned or unplanned, no matter what her age, most women experience hormonal changes that cause them to be easily upset during pregnancy.

> *Brooke had an attitude while she was pregnant. She had the flashes. I guess that's normal, but in the end it boiled down to I needed to help her stay calm. It was difficult, because she had the emotions, "Is he cheating? Is he doing this or that?" We had to get through that.*
>
> Joel, 19 - Blair, 3 months

In addition to these physical changes, your partner may
have other problems. Her parents may be upset about the
pregnancy. She may find it difficult to continue her education. The future may look pretty scary. Your support could
help her cope with these feelings.

## She Needs a Labor Coach

*I was with her in the delivery room. I tripped out.*
*When I first saw Gus coming out, when I saw his*
*head, it was weird.*

*I stayed at the hospital with them for the two days,*
*and we had the baby in the room with us. The nurse*
*showed us how to sponge bathe him, how not to get*
*the cord wet, how to make bottles, how to clean him*
*and change him, and how to keep him wrapped up.*
*She kept coming in to ask if we needed help.*

                                        Andy, 17 - Gus, 5 months


Thinking about her approaching labor and delivery may
be frightening for your partner. Taking a prepared childbirth
class together would help you both prepare for the big task
of getting your baby born. At these classes, you'll learn
how you can act as her "coach" for the big event.

If you are her labor coach, you'll encourage her to
breathe in certain ways during her contractions and to focus
on a specific point as she labors. Rubbing her back or
simply letting her hold your hand during her contractions
will help. Your prepared childbirth teacher will advise you
of other ways you can be involved in the birth of
your child.

Research shows a father who is with his partner when
their baby is born is likely to be closer to the mother and
baby a year later than are fathers who were not involved in
their child's birth.

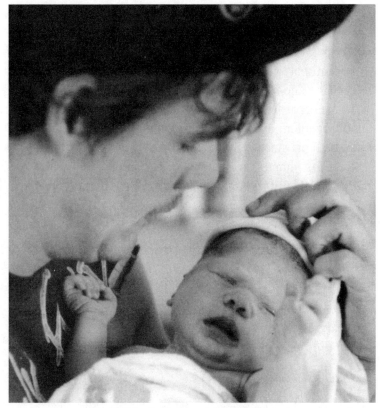

*He and his dad are great friends already.*

*At first I didn't like her being pregnant because I*
*was too young. Then after I saw her have the baby*
*and they let me cut the cord, joy came to me. I got*
*happy, and tears started coming out of my eyes.*
Leandro, 17 - Jonathan, 18 months

Sometimes fathers have jealous feelings after their baby is born. Your partner may seem totally absorbed in the baby and have no time left for you. Perhaps she seems exhausted much of the time. Your best defense is to be as involved as possible with her in caring for your child.

As your baby's father, you can do everything for your

newborn that his mother can do except breastfeed. If she's
breastfeeding, you can bring baby to her at night, change
his diaper, cuddle him . . . and *enjoy* him. You can be a very
important part of baby's life from the beginning. If you are,
you, baby, and mom will *all* win.

If she plans to breastfeed your baby, she'll need your
encouragement and support. Together, you can give your
baby the best start in life.

Reading chapter 11, especially if you're living with your
baby's mother, will guide you in helping her and your new
baby get started with breastfeeding.

## You're Responsible

*Before delivery I took everything out of my room
that I didn't need so I could make space for the crib
and stroller and other things for the baby. Whitney
picked out the color, and I painted the room. Whitney
got a lot of things at her baby shower, and that helped
a lot.*

Randy

Randy knew he needed to stay in school. Dropping out
and trying to support his family at a minimum pay job
didn't make sense. There were other ways he could be
responsible right now.

Even if you can't offer much financial support now, you
can be involved in the care of your child. Do your share
of baby care. Perhaps your parents can provide some
child care.

If you're both in school, you may need to set up a schedule for child care which will allow time for each of you to
do your homework.

Do you have health insurance? If so, check to see if it
covers your baby too.

## It's Not Easy

Andy speaks for many teen fathers when he discusses the difficulties of having a child before he was ready:

> *The hard thing is you're still a kid and you can't deny it. There's nothing you can do about it. You got yourself into this mess. I wish I had never had kids because there are a lot of things I'd like to be doing now. But you can't change what you've done. You have to deal with it even though there are times when you say, "This sucks." You see a lot of your friends who don't have kids, and you wish you were like them.*
>
> *Now I have to think about my baby when I'm walking on the street, and it feels weird. Before, I didn't have anyone to think about except myself. Now I have to watch out for all three of us. It's hard.*
>
> Andy, 17 - Gus, 5 months

Of course it's hard. Parenting a child is one of the most difficult — and one of the most rewarding — tasks faced by human beings. Getting pregnant before she's ready changes a young woman's life tremendously. It also drastically changes her baby's father's life.

Teen fathers who hang in there, who choose to face the great responsibility of supporting and actively parenting their child, may face hardship and broken dreams just as their baby's mother does. When you choose this route, you also can look forward to the joys of seeing your baby grow, first into a charming and independent toddler, then through childhood and on to becoming the responsible, mature adult you want him to be.

*What a wonderful challenge!*

*Delaying the second pregnancy means more time and attention
for your first baby — and a greater chance to reach your own goals.*

# 14

# Another Baby — When?

*I hadn't planned to get pregnant, but we were kind of stupid about it. We didn't use a condom or anything. My friend had been doing it for a year and she didn't get pregnant, so I didn't think I would. We weren't together very long. Through everything we've been off and on. I'm six months pregnant now, and we've broken up many times while I've been pregnant.*

Libbey, 15, 6 months pregnant

*I've told my boyfriend I don't want to get pregnant again, and that I'm going to take care of myself. We talked, and he agrees.*

Christina, pregnant at 15

Many teen mothers get pregnant again soon after the birth of their first child. In fact, more than half are pregnant within two years after their first delivery.

Is this what you want? Or would you rather wait a while longer before getting pregnant again? Reasons you might like to wait include:

- Being able to give your first child the attention and care s/he needs. Toddlers need as much attention, although of a different kind, as infants.

- Your body is less likely to produce a healthy baby if your pregnancies are too close together.

- More babies usually mean more poverty.

- With one child, you may be able to find childcare so you can continue school and work toward your other goals. With two children, it would be much harder.

- Your relationship with your partner is likely to suffer if you have too many children too close together.

If you would prefer to delay your next pregnancy, are you planning now how you'll achieve that goal?

Of course no one *has* to be sexually active. Abstinence from sexual activity permits the couple to explore their relationship in many other ways.

---

**Abstinence:** Not having sexual intercourse

---

## Sex May Change Relationship

Sexual activity is both physical and emotional. The emotional part of sexual intercourse may be quite different for each partner.

Sometimes one partner holds the power in a relationship because the other person has such strong emotions concerning the sexual act. This power can have an important effect on the relationship.

Generally, neither partner feels the same after they begin having sexual intercourse. That can be good, or it can cause serious differences between the two. Pregnancy further complicates things.

During pregnancy is a good time to think about family planning. You can't get pregnant again quite yet, so you have time to look at your options with little risk.

## Issues to Consider

Several issues are involved in contraceptive decision-making:

- Some people think the girl who "takes precautions" is not a "nice" girl.

- A woman who has been in an unhappy relationship may truly feel she'll never be in a sexual relationship again.

- Women often feel the contraceptive decision should be made between partners.

First, the "nice girl" issue. If she isn't ready to have a baby, not getting pregnant is a responsible approach, an approach that appears mature and caring. Aren't nice girls mature and caring?

A woman who carries condoms with her is showing her partner that she cares about herself, her future, and his. That's being a nice girl!

Second, the teen who doesn't plan ever to have sexual intercourse again may be sincere. However, a teenager has about thirty years of fertility left. She is likely to need family planning information at some time during those years.

Third, the issue of the partners deciding together. The fact is that many couples find it extremely difficult to talk

about sex at all. Discussing family planning at length is
even harder.

*Most of my friends, who are already teen moms,
are afraid to say, "Use a condom" to their partners.
They know about it, but the barrier is trying to talk to
your partner. Sometimes they talk about it, and the
partner says, "No, I won't use it." Then they give up.
I think they need to take care of themselves because of
the babies they have now.*

Angelica, pregnant at 17

Some young women say their partners don't want them
to use birth control. One student even told us her boyfriend
wouldn't "let" her use birth control because he thought if
she did, she might have sex with other guys. A relationship
with so little trust between the partners appears to be in
trouble. If she's going to continue to have sex with this
boyfriend, this young woman might decide to use a
contraceptive in spite of his objections.

## Other Objections to Contraception

Other objections to using contraception include:

- "I can't afford it." (Babies cost more than
  contraception.)
- "I don't have transportation to the clinic." (Keeping
  your prenatal care appointments takes transportation
  too.)
- My mother might find out. (Your mother will notice
  when you're eight months pregnant.)

The person who can get pregnant surely should have the
right to decide whether she wants to be pregnant or not. If
she doesn't, she needs either to abstain from sex or use an

effective contraceptive.

The doctor will usually discuss birth control with you at your six-weeks postpartum checkup. Be sure you keep this appointment, and be prepared with questions. Remember that medical staff is not there to judge you or anyone else. They will be happy to give you information and assistance. It's their job, and they like to think their work counts. They probably feel strongly that planned children are preferable.

## Lots of Options

There is a wide variety of contraceptive devices. Each person needs to consider what's available, then decide which is best for her/him. People who don't feel comfortable touching their genitals may prefer a type of protection which they don't have to insert themselves. See the "systemics" below.

**Barriers:** Condom, diaphragm, cervical cap

**Spermicides:** Jelly, foam, suppositories

**Systemics:** Birth control pills, hormone injections, contraceptive implant, patch, vaginal ring

**IUD:** Intrauterine device

**Abstinence:** Not having vaginal, oral, or rectal sex

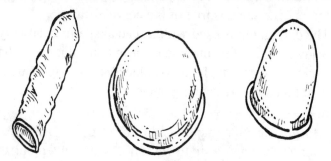

*Condom, diaphragm, cervical cap*

Several contraceptives do not require a prescription, and you can buy them in almost any drugstore. These include spermicidal jelly or foam, the condom (both male and female), and suppositories. All of them kill sperm or prevent them from getting into the uterus.

These methods also help prevent the spread of sexually transmitted infections (STIs). The condom does this best, but the other products kill some germs.

Spermicides used alone as a contraceptive have a high failure rate. If used perfectly, the user has a 4 percent chance of getting pregnant the first year. Typical use, however, raises the failure rate to 26 percent.

If you're using a spermicide (foam, cream, suppositories, film), your partner should also use a condom each time you have intercourse.

The man needs to put the condom on carefully *before* he has any sexual contact with his partner. It will feel more comfortable to him and be less likely to break if he leaves about one-half inch of space at the end as he puts it on his erect penis.

The diaphragm is a molded rubber cup that is placed in the vagina to keep the sperm from getting into the uterus. You need to see a doctor to be fitted for a diaphragm. If you had one before your baby was born, you will need a new one afterward since the size of your cervix may be different. The same is true of the cervical cap.

The diaphragm is used with a special spermicidal jelly. The advantage of this method of birth control is that it has few to no side effects. It can be placed in the vagina up to several hours before sexual contact.

**Important:** the diaphragm, to be effective, needs to be left in the vagina six to eight hours after intercourse.

The newer vaginal ring stays in place for three weeks. It does contain hormones. When you take it out after three weeks, you throw it away and replace it with a new ring. Cost of the vaginal ring is about $38 (still cheaper than one pregnancy).

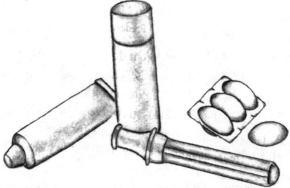

*Contraceptive jelly, foam, and suppositories*

Suppositories are small waxlike pellets that are placed in the vagina before sexual contact. They melt at body temperature, releasing a sperm-killing substance.

A suppository contraceptive is effective for about six hours. If, after six hours, you're going to have intercourse, you need to insert another suppository.

Items such as the condom, foam, and jelly are sometimes available free at your local health department. The effects of foam and jelly are temporary. They must be used at or near the time of sexual contact.

## Birth Control Pill

Birth control pills are widely available from doctors and clinics. Insurance or Medicaid pays for this service. The advantage of the pill is that it doesn't have to be used at the time of sexual intercourse. You do have to be sure you take one every day.

*If you don't have someone there to remind you, you*
*can forget about it. Tyson reminds me. We never*
*talked about birth control before I got pregnant. I*
*didn't think it would happen to me — but it did.*

Frederica, 16 - Jesse, 5 months

The pill is available in different doses. Even if you've taken
it before and weren't happy with
it, talk with your healthcare
provider again. She might
suggest a different dosage for
you.

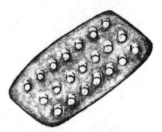

Usually a person gets a six-
month supply of the pill. Some

*Birth control pill*

women have some side effects during the first month after
they start taking the pill. Seldom does this last any longer.

Note: The pill will not keep you from getting
pregnant the first month you take it. Neither is the pill
effective if you're taking antibiotics. If you have sex
during that first month or while you're on antibiotics,
use another contraceptive.

Taking the pill may cut back on a breastfeeding mother's
supply of milk. If you're breastfeeding, talk to your doctor.
You might prefer to use another contraceptive while you're
breastfeeding.

## Intrauterine Device (IUD)

The IUD (Intrauterine Device) is a
plastic device about an inch long, and
comes in various shapes. It is placed in
the uterus by the doctor during a pelvic
examination. Once there, it stays in for

*IUD*

*Some people delay their second pregnancy
because they want more time with their first child.*

several years.

The IUD is recommended only for women who have had a child and who are in a sexual relationship with only one person. The risk of infection from the IUD increases if the person has several partners.

## Birth Control Injections

Injectable medication, such as Depo Provera, is a contraceptive alternative that differs from the other methods. You are given a shot which is effective in preventing pregnancy for three months (99 percent effective). Advantages of injectables include:

- You don't have to remember to take anything daily.

- It is appropriate for people who can't take the pill.

- Breastfeeding women can have the injection at their six-week postpartum visit. However, if you're planning to continue breastfeeding, it would be best to choose a different method of contraception.

If you use an injectable, be sure you schedule an appointment with your doctor every three months for your injection.

*Taisha was using the Depo-Provera shot, but I think she was late in getting her shot. The pregnancy was a big surprise. My mother set me down and talked to me. She made me understand there would have to be changes in my life.*

Saunders, 17 - Trilby, 1 year

## Contraceptive Patch, Implant

The patch provides preventive hormones through the skin. It is a 11/2" x 11/2" patch which you place on your skin for seven days, then remove. Place a new patch on your skin for another week, remove again. Put a third patch on your skin, and remove in a week. *Do this on the same day each week.* Then you'll have a period without wearing a patch. When your period is over, you repeat the process. Continue as long as you wish to avoid pregnancy.

Another family planning device is the implant. It is a low dose of birth control medicine in a capsule. The doctor puts the capsule under the skin of the patient's upper arm. It doesn't show.

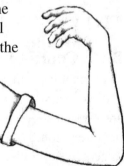

Once there, it slowly releases the pregnancy-preventing medicine. This continues for at least one year. Some may prevent pregnancy for five years. Your insurance may cover the cost of the implant.

*Contraceptive implant*

If you decide you want the implant removed, your healthcare provider can do so.

## Emergency Contraception

If, in spite of good planning, unprotected sexual intercourse occurs, it is possible for the woman to see her healthcare provider for emergency contraception. There are medications that prevent pregnancy *if taken within 72 hours after intercourse.* They are 75 percent effective.

The emergency contraception pills have some mild side effects, but *much* less than pregnancy. The best plan is for you to use a condom and the woman to use another form of contraception *always.*

But don't despair if the unexpected occurs. For more information on one type of emergency contraception, call 1.888.PREVEN 2 (1.888.773.8362).

You might want to ask your healthcare provider for a prescription for emergency contraception so you'll have it on hand if necessary. In some states you can buy it on line, www.NOT-2-LATE.com>

## Pregnancy Testing

If you think you're pregnant, get tested right away. Pregnancy tests are available without a prescription. Read the directions carefully since they are not all alike. Many women think they're pregnant, but are not. They stop using protection, and the next month they conceive.

*Ovulation* tests are often displayed next to the pregnancy testing kits. They do not tell you if you're pregnant, so be sure you get the *pregnancy* test.

If you don't want to be pregnant again soon, make plans to prevent pregnancy. Choose not to have sex or, if you're having sex, use birth control — always.

## STI Concerns

*Be careful about sex, and make sure you know*
*what you're doing. Really take care of yourself. If you*
*don't use a condom, you'd better. Get those AIDS*
*tests and make sure you don't have STIs, because*
*those things can affect your baby.*

                                    Emilia, 17 - Sancia, 6 months

Sexually active people also need to be concerned about
sexually transmitted infections (STIs). Some of these
conditions, such as a yeast infection, are merely annoying.
Others have much more long-lasting effects and need
immediate treatment. AIDS causes death.

Using a condom is quite effective in the transmission of
these infections. It's even better if a spermicidal jelly is
used with the condom.

Although the risk is greater with vaginal and rectal sex,
STIs can also be passed from one partner to the other
through oral sex. Using a dental dam, household plastic
wrap, or a split, flattened, unlubricated condom during oral
sex provides some protection.

Remember that, as far as STIs are concerned, when you
have sexual intercourse, you're having sex with everyone
with whom your partner has ever had sex. If your partner
caught an STI from a former partner, s/he can give you
the disease.

If you ever have any of the following symptoms, even if
you haven't had sexual intercourse for awhile, see your
healthcare provider or go to a clinic:
- Painful urination (both men and women)
- Unusual discharge from the penis or vagina
- Sore or itching genitals (sex organs)
- Lumps or growths around genital areas
- Rashes or blisters on the genital area

• Sores on the penis, on the vulva, or in the vagina

---
**Vulva:** Female outside sex area

---

Remember: Most sexually transmitted infections can be treated without serious lifelong effects *if* you see the doctor soon enough. Medicaid and private insurance pay for this type of care.

STIs should be treated in both partners. Birth defects, prematurity, and fetal death can result from untreated HIV, syphilis, and gonorrhea. Other untreated infections also contribute to prematurity.

Public health departments are especially good at providing free or very low cost treatment for STIs.

## AIDS — The Incurable STI

The one exception to that statement about successful treatment is AIDS. AIDS stands for Acquired Immune Deficiency Syndrome. The AIDS virus makes the body unable to resist diseases. A person with AIDS could die from any disease, but usually cancer or pneumonia is the cause of death.

There are no early symptoms *and no cure* for this disease. People who have AIDS can be given care for the symptoms, and many live for years with treatment. However, they will not be cured.

In the past some people have gotten AIDS through blood transfusions, but this is almost impossible today because of improved testing of blood.

Today people get AIDS by:

• Having sex with an infected person.

• Sharing needles or syringes with infected people who use any intravenous drugs.

• Having sex with someone who shares needles with IV drug users.

• Before birth from his/her mother.

## Caring for Yourself and Your Family

Remember that the more partners you have, the more likely you are to get a sexually transmitted infection. Think about other ways to have a loving relationship. Delay sex until you know your partner well. Discuss protection from pregnancy before you begin the sexual part of the relationship. Consider the risks that both pregnancy and sexually transmitted infections may present to you and your partner.

---

*About half of all couples who have unprotected intercourse a dozen times will become pregnant.*

---

The best protection against infections and unintended pregnancy is for each partner to use protection. Whatever the method the woman uses, the man should *always* use a condom to protect both partners against STIs.

The pregnancy prevention failure rate for condoms used alone is, for the first year, 3 percent with "perfect" use, and 14 percent with "typical" use. To protect both partners from unplanned pregnancy, the woman should also use a birth control method such as the pill, contraceptive implant, or injectable.

Having your next child when you and your partner are physically, emotionally, and financially ready is better for your present child and your future family. It's up to you and your partner to make this happen. And if your partner isn't interested, *it's up to you.*

# APPENDIX

# About the Authors

Jean Brunelli, PHN, has worked with hundreds of pregnant teenagers. For fifteen years she taught prenatal health and parenting in the Teen Parent Program, ABC Unified School

District, Cerritos, California.

A school nurse, she was the director for ten years of the Tracy Infant and Toddler Program for Children with Special Needs and Their Families. Jean is also active in and an officer of the Infant Development Association of California.

Jean is a graduate of Mt. St. Mary's College, Los Angeles. She and Mike have two grown children, one granddaughter and one grandson.

Jeanne Warren Lindsay is the author of seventeen other books dealing with adolescent pregnancy and parenting. She, too, has worked with hundreds of pregnant and parenting teenagers. She developed the Teen Parent Program at Tracy High School, Cerritos, California, and coordinated/taught in the program for sixteen years. She continued as a consultant for six more years. Currently, she maintains her ties with teens through the interviews she conducts for her books.

She has completed graduate degrees in Anthropology and Family and Consumer Science. She and Bob have five grown children and seven grandchildren.

# BIBLIOGRAPHY

The following bibliography, updated in 2003, contains books and a few other resources for pregnant and parenting teens and those who work with them. Workbooks and other classroom aids are available for many titles.

If the resource is available on Amazon or other on-line bookstore, only the publisher's name is listed. If not, the publisher's address and phone number are listed, but only with the first resource described from that publisher.

Prices quoted were current July, 2003, but prices tend to change. If you can't find a book in your bookstore, you can usually get it directly from the publisher. Enclose $3 for shipping per book. See pages 223-224 for an order form for Morning Glory Press publications.

Anasar, Eleanor. **"You and Your Baby: Playing and Learning Together." "You and Your Baby: A Special Relationship."** 2001. **"You and Your Baby: The Toddler Years."** 2003. 32 pp. each. Each available in English and Spanish editions. $2.65 each. Bulk discounts. The Corner Health Center, 47 North Huron Street, Ypsilanti, MI 48197. 734.484.3600.

*Gorgeous photos of teen parents and their children on every other page. Each booklet contains helpful information at an extremely easy reading level.*

Arnoldi, Katherine. **The Amazing True Story of a Teenage Single Mom.** 1998. 176 pp. $16. Hyperion.
*Written in a true experience/comic book format, it's the story of a young mom who had dreams, but faced many obstacles in fulfilling them.*

Arthur, Shirley. **Surviving Teen Pregnancy: Your Choices, Dreams and Decisions.** 1996. 192 pp. $11.95. Teacher/Study Guides, $2.50/ set. Morning Glory Press, 6595 San Haroldo Way, Buena Park, CA 90620. 714.828.1998, 888.612.8254.
*Helps pregnant teens understand their alternatives. Offers guidance in learning decision-making. Chapter on adoption planning is included.*

Barr, Linda, M.N., and Catherine Monserrat, Ph.D. **Teenage Pregnancy: A New Beginning.** Revised 2002. 151 pp. Spiral binding, $18.95. Workbook, $4.95. New Futures, Inc., 4919 Prospect NE, Albuquerque, NM 87110. 505.872.0164.
*Prenatal health book written specifically for pregnant adolescents. Spans the childbearing cycle from conception through early parenthood.*

Beaglehole, Ruth. **Mama, listen! Raising a Child without Violence: A Handbook for Teen Parents.** 1998. 224 pp. $25. Curriculum Guide, $20. Ruth Beaglehole, 2162 Echo Park Ave., Los Angeles, CA 90026. 323.661.9123.
*A unique book. Most of it is written as if a toddler is speaking, explaining what s/he needs from his/her parents. Good description of emotional needs of small children. An absolute lack of violence (**no** spanking) is recommended throughout.*

Brinkley, Ginny, and Sherry Sampson. **Baby and Me: A Pregnancy Workbook for Young Women.** 1997. 44 pp. $3. ICEA, P.O. Box 20048. 951.854.8660.
*Reader-friendly overview of pregnancy, labor, and birth written especially for teens. Simply written, cartoon illustrations.*

_____. Illus. by Gail Spratt Cooper. **You and Your New Baby — A Book for Young Mothers.** Also in Spanish: **Usted y su nuevo bebé.** 1996. 80 pp. $3. ICEA.
*Simple and complete guide for caring for baby. Written in a format for easy understanding.*

_____. **Young and Pregnant — A Book For You.** Also in Spanish: **Joven y embarazada.** 1995. 73 pp. $3. ICEA

*Refreshingly simple book on prenatal care directed to teenagers. Provides basic information. Also available in condensed 48-page version,* **Promises: A Teen's Guide to Pregnancy.** *1993. $2.*

Coles, Robert. **The Youngest Parents: Teenage Pregnancy as It Shapes Lives.** 2000. 224 pp. $19.99. W. W. Norton and Company, 800.233.4830.

*An absorbing book which offers the compelling voices of young women and men, either pregnant or already parents, to provide yet another dimension to the realities of teen parents' lives. Includes nearly 100 pages of wonderful black and white photos.*

**Complete Teens Parenting Curriculum.** 2002. Includes two books, five *Comprehensive Curriculum Notebooks,* and quarterly newsletter for teacher; and, for students, six books and workbooks *(Teens Parenting* Series), eight videos, four games. $1085. Morning Glory Press. 888.612.8254.

*Everything you need to teach parenting to teen parents. See descriptions of Teens Parenting books, games, videos, pp. 217-219.*

Eisenberg, Arlene, Heidi E. Murkoff, and Sandee E. Hathaway, B.S.N. **What to Expect When You're Expecting.** 2002. 624 pp. $13.95. Workman Publishing.

*Discusses prenatal diagnosis, childbirth options, second pregnancies, twins, Cesarean birth, practical tips on coping with pregnancy symptoms. Step-by-step guides through labor and delivery, postpartum care, breastfeeding.*

Fenwick, Elizabeth, et al. **How Sex Works: A Clear, Comprehensive Guide for Teenagers to Emotional, Physical, and Sexual Maturity.** 1996. 96 pp. $9.95. Dorling Kindersley Pub., Inc. 877.342.5357.
*Profusely illustrated, easy-to-read comprehensive guide for teenagers to emotional, physical, and sexual maturity.*

Goldberg, Linda, Ginny Brinkley, Janice Kukar. **Pregnancy to Parenthood.** 2001. 342 pp. $12.95. Avery Penguin Putnam. 800.548.5757.
*Provides month-by-month breakdown of physical changes to expect during pregnancy, describes the emotional aspects of pregnancy, and much more.*

**Guidance for the Journey: A Pregnancy Journal.** 2000. CD, $100. Booklet, 2002, $6. Face to Face Health & Counseling Service, Inc., Doreen Williams, 1165 Arcade, St. Paul, MN 55106. 651.772.5555.
*Software program which produces personalized pregnancy journals.*

Harris, Robie H. Illus. by Michael Emberley. **It's Perfectly Normal: Changing Bodies, Growing Up, Sex and Sexual Health.** 1996. 89 pp. $10.99. Candlewick Press.

*The illustrations are wonderful, and make it difficult to continue thinking of sex as something we never talk about with our children.*

Hatcher, Robert A., et al. ***A Personal Guide to Managing Contraception.*** 2000. 179 pp. $14.95. Bridging the Gap Communications. 706.265.3912.
*Remarkably complete and medically accurate coverage of the various contraceptive methods. Good resource for teens.*

***Heart to Heart Program.*** For information, Heart to Heart, Ounce of Prevention Fund, 122 South Michigan Avenue, Ste. 2050, Chicago, IL 60603. 312.922.3863.
*An innovative approach to preventing child sexual abuse by teaching teen parents to protect their children from abuse. Program can be implemented in a school or community-based setting. Practitioners participate in a two-day training and purchase the curriculum and facilitator's guide.*

Humenick, Sharon S. ***Having a Baby.*** 1997. 96 pp. $9.75. New Readers Press, Box 35888, Syracuse, NY 13235. 800.448.8878.
*Provides a quick guide to pregnancy and childbirth. Very easy-to-read. Provides good overview, but not much detail.*

***It Takes Two: For Teen Parents.*** 1997. 124 pp. Teachers Manual, $50; 26-page Student Manual, $6. Legacy Resource Group, P.O. Box 700, Carlisle, IA 50047. 515.989.3360.
*It's a five-hour pregnancy prevention curriculum for teen parents. Encourages participants to look at their own values and their dreams, and to discuss how parenting has impacted those dreams. Emphasizes shared responsibility between men and women.*

Jacobs, Thomas A., et al. ***What Are My Rights? 95 Questions and Answers about Teens and the Law.*** 1997. 208 pp. $14.95. Free Spirit Publishing. 612.338.2068.
*A matter-of-fact guide to the laws that affect teens at home, at school, on the job, and in their communities.*

Leach, Penelope. ***Your Baby and Child from Birth to Age Five.*** Revised, 1997. 560 pp. $20. Alfred A. Knopf.
*An absolutely beautiful book packed with information, many color photos and lovely drawings. Comprehensive, authoritative, and outstandingly sensitive guide to child care and development.*

Lerman, Evelyn. ***Safer Sex: The New Morality.*** 2000. 240 pp. Paper, $14.95; hardcover, $21.95. Adult Leader's Guide, $5. Participant's

Guide, $2.50. Morning Glory Press.

*Safer Sex provides an honest appraisal of the impact of unprotected sex on the lives of teens, along with proven strategies for positive change. Wonderful guide for parents, teachers, clergy, counselors, all who love, care and worry about teens in our world of free sex in the media and our passion for keeping teens away from sex in the real world.*

_____. *Teen Moms: The Pain and the Promise.* 1997. 192 pp. Paper, $14.95; hardcover, $21.95. Workbook, T.G., $2.50 each. Adult Leader's Guide, $5. Participant's Guide, $2.50. Morning Glory.

*Stories from teen moms together with illuminating research. Especially good for board members and others who don't know much about the realities of teen parents' lives. Offers good background material for people working on teen pregnancy prevention.*

Lieberman, E. James, M.D., and Karen Lieberman Troccoli, M.P.H. *Like It Is: A Teen Sex Guide.* 1998. 216 pp. $25. McFarland and Co.

*Excellent book to offer teen parents (all teens actually). It describes methods of contraception, starting with abstinence, and the risks associated with each one. Gives bias-free information about pregnancy options.*

Lindsay, Jeanne Warren. *The Challenge of Toddlers* and *Your Baby's First Year (Teens Parenting Series).* 2004. 224 pp. each. Paper, $12.95 each; hardcover, $18.95 each. Workbooks, $2.50 each. Morning Glory Press. 888.612.8254.

*How-to-parent books especially for teenage parents. Lots of quotes from teenage parents who share their experiences. Board games ($29.95 each), one for each of these titles, provide great learning reinforcement. Also available is a 4-video series, Your Baby's First Year. For detailed teaching guide, see Challenge of Toddlers Comprehensive Curriculum Notebook and Nurturing Your Newborn/Your Baby's First Year Comprehensive Curriculum Notebook below.*

_____. **Five *Comprehensive Curriculum Notebooks* for *Teens Parenting Series: Your Pregnancy and Newborn Journey; Nurturing Your Newborn/Your Baby's First Year; The Challenge of Toddlers; Discipline from Birth to Three; Teen Dads.*** 2002. 175-190 pp. loose-leaf notebooks. $125 each; 5/$500. Morning Glory.

*Each notebook contains, for each chapter of book, objectives, supplementary resources, teacher tips, group and independent study activities list, reproducible activities, handout listing high points of chapter, quiz, answer key, and suggested responses for all workbook assignments.*

_____. *Do I Have a Daddy? A Story About a Single-Parent Child.*

2000. 48 pp. Paper, $7.95; hardcover, $14.95. Free study guide.
Morning Glory Press.
*A beautiful full-color picture book for the child who has never met his/her father. A special sixteen-page section offers suggestions to single mothers.*

_____. ***Pregnant? Adoption Is an Option.*** 1996. 224 pp. $11.95.
Teacher's Guide, Study Guide, $2.50 each. Morning Glory Press.
*Birthparents share stories of responsible, difficult adoption planning. Does not "push" adoption, but suggests **planning** and deliberate decision-making. Stresses open adoption and birthparents' role in choosing adoptive parents.*

_____. ***Teen Dads: Rights, Responsibilities and Joys (Teens Parenting* Series)**. 2001. 224 pp. $12.95. Teacher's Guide, Workbook, $2.50 each. Morning Glory Press.
*A how-to-parent book especially for teenage fathers. Offers help in parenting from conception to age 3 of the child. Many quotes from and photos of teen fathers. For detailed teaching help, see **Teen Dads Comprehensive Curriculum Notebook** on previous page.*

_____. ***Teenage Couples — Caring, Commitment and Change: How to Build a Relationship that Lasts. Teenage Couples — Coping with Reality: Dealing with Money, In-laws, Babies and Other Details of Daily Life.*** 1995. 208, 192 pp. Paper, $9.95 ea.; hardcover, $15.95 ea. Workbooks, $2.50 ea. Curriculum Guide, $19.95. Morning Glory Press.
*Series covers such important topics as communication, handling arguments, keeping romance alive, sex in a relationship, jealousy, alcohol and drug addiction, partner abuse, and divorce, as well as the practical details of living. Lots of quotes from teenage couples.*

_____. ***Your Pregnancy and Newborn Journey Comprehensive Curriculum Notebook.*** Morning Glory. See description on p. 217.
*Also available are two games developed by Diane Smallwood: **Pregnancy and Newborn Journey Board Game** ($29.95) and **Two-in-One Pregnancy Bingo** ($19.95). Wonderful learning and review resources.*

_____ and Jean Brunelli. ***Nurturing Your Newborn: Young Parent's Guide to Baby's First Month.*** *(Teens Parenting Series)* 1999. 64 pp. $6.95. Morning Glory.
*Focuses on the postpartum period. Ideal for teen parents home after delivery. For detailed teaching help, see **Nurturing Your Newborn/Your Baby's First Year Comprehensive Curriculum Notebook** on p. 217.*

_____ and Sharon Enright. ***Books, Babies and School-Age Parents: How to Help Pregnant and Parenting Teens Succeed.*** 1997. 288 pp. $14.95. Morning Glory Press.

*Help in understanding special issues of teenage parents and working more effectively with this special population.*

_____ and Sally McCullough. **Discipline from Birth to Three**. 2004. 208 pp. Paper, $12.95; hardcover, $18.95. Morning Glory Press.
*Provides teenage parents with guidelines to help prevent discipline problems with children and for dealing with problems when they occur. For detailed teaching help, see Discipline from Birth to Three Comprehensive Curriculum Notebook, p. 217.*

Marecek, Mary. **Breaking Free from Partner Abuse**. 1999. 96 pp. $8.95. Quantity discount. Morning Glory Press.
*Lovely edition illustrated by Jami Moffett. Underlying message is that the reader does not deserve to be hit. Simply written. Can help a young woman escape an abusive relationship.*

Morris, Jon. **ROAD to Fatherhood: How to Help Young Dads Become Loving and Responsible Parents**. 2002. 208 pp. $14.95. Morning Glory Press.
*Book shows the many needs of young fathers through their real stories together with strategies for helping them meet their individual and unique challenges. Also excellent planning guide for starting or expanding a program for young fathers.*

Nykiel, Connie. **After the Loss of Your Baby — For Teen Mothers**. 1994. 19 pp. $4.50 ppd. Spanish edition, *Despues de la Perdida de tu Bebé: Para Madres Adolescentes*. Centering Corp., 7230 Maple St., Omaha, NE 68134. 402.553.1200.
*Tremendous resource. Beautifully written to help teens through grief of losing a baby, whether through miscarriage, stillbirth, SIDS, or other death.*

Pollock, Sudie. **Moving On: Finding Information You Need for Living on Your Own**. 2001. 48 pp. $4.95. 25/$75. Morning Glory Press.
*Fill-in guide to help young persons find information about their community, information needed for living away from parents.*

_____. **Will the Dollars Stretch? Teen Parents Living on Their Own**. 2001. 112 pp. $7.95. Teacher's Guide, $2.50. Morning Glory.
*Five short stories about teen parents moving out on their own. As students read, they will get the feel of poverty as experienced by many teen parents — as they write checks and balance checkbooks of young parents involved.*

**Parents as Teachers National Center, Inc.** 10176 Corporate Square Drive, Ste. 230, St. Louis, MO 63132. 314.432.4330.
*PAT is an early childhood parent education and family support program designed to empower all parents to give their child the best possible start in*

*life. "Issues in Working with Teen Parents" is specially designed training for professionals working with teen parents and their young children.*

Porter, Connie. *Imani All Mine.* 1999. 218 pp. $12. Houghton Miflin.
*Wonderful novel about a black teen mom in the ghetto where poverty, racism, and danger are constant realities.*

Renfrew, May, Chloe Fisher, and Suzanne Arms. *Bestfeeding: Getting Breastfeeding Right for You.* 2000. 272 pp. $14.95. Celestial Arts Publishing, P.O. Box 7123, Berkeley, CA 94707. 800.841.2665.
*Marvelous description, with lots of photographs and drawings (150+) of the importance of breastfeeding, and of how to make the process work. Wonderful resource for teacher. While many students may not want to read the whole book, simply looking at the photos and drawings could be helpful.*

Reynolds, Marilyn. **True-to-Life Series from Hamilton High.** *Detour for Emmy. Telling. Too Soon for Jeff. Beyond Dreams. Baby Help. But What About Me? Love Rules. If You Loved Me.* 1993-2001. 160-256 pp. Paper, $8.95 each (*Love Rules,* $9.95). *True to Life Series Teaching Guide (*1996, 144 pp, $21.95) covers first four titles. Separate guide available for each of the other four books. $2.50 each. Morning Glory Press.
*Wonderfully gripping stories about situations faced by teens. Start with* **Detour for Emmy,** *award-winning novel about a 15-year-old mother. Students who read one of Reynolds' novels usually ask for more. Topics cover partner abuse, acquaintance rape, reluctant teen father, sexual molestation, racism, fatal accident, abstinence, homophobia, school failure.*

Romanchik, Brenda. **The Open Adoption Pocket Guide Book Series: *Being a Birthparent: Finding Our Place; What Is Open Adoption? Your Rights and Responsibilities: A Guide for Expectant Parents Considering Adoption;* and *Birthparent Grief.*** 1999. 20 pp. ea. $5.95 ea. R-Squared Press.
*Concise guides filled with usable information. Excellent for educating family and friends.*

Wiggins, Pamela K. *Why Should I Nurse My Baby?* 1998. 58 pp. $5.95. Noodle Soup, 4614 Prospect Avenue, #328, Cleveland, OH 44103. 216.881.5151.
*Easy-to-read, yet thorough discussion of breastfeeding. Question and answer format. Also ask about the* **Babies First** *pamphlets, same source.*

Wolff, Virginia E. *Make Lemonade.* 2003. 208 pp. $5.99. Scholastic.
*Wonderful novel about a teenager living in a Project who takes a job babysitting for a teenage mom, and who eventually sees the mom back in school, her children in child care, and her life back on focus.*

# INDEX

Morning Glory Press
6595 San Haroldo Way, Buena Park, CA 90620
714.828.1998; 888.612.8254  Fax 714.828.2049
*Contact us for complete catalog including quantity and other discounts.*

|  |  | Price | Total |
|---|---|---|---|
| __ *Complete* **Teens Parenting Curriculum** | | $1085.00 | _____ |

One each — Five *Comprehensive Curriculum Notebooks*
plus 8 books, 6 workbooks, 8 videos, 4 games
(everything on this order form except last 13 titles as noted on p. 2)
**Buy a text and workbook for each student.**
**Contact us for generous quantity discounts.**

---

### Resources for Teen Parent Teachers/Counselors:

| | | | |
|---|---|---|---|
| __ *Books, Babies and School-Age Parents* | | | |
| | 1-885356-22-6 | 14.95 | _____ |
| __ *ROAD to Fatherhood* | 1-885356-92-7 | 14.95 | _____ |

### Resources for Teen Parents:

| | | | |
|---|---|---|---|
| *Your Pregnancy and Newborn Journey* | | | |
| — Paper | 1-932538-00-3 | 12.95 | _____ |
| — Hardcover | 1-932538-01-1 | 18.95 | _____ |
| — Workbook | 1-932538-02-x | 2.50 | _____ |
| __ *PNJ Curriculum Notebook* | 1-885356-96-x | 125.00 | _____ |
| __ **PNJ Board Game** | 1-885356-19-6 | 29.95 | _____ |
| __ **Pregnancy Two-in-One Bingo** | 1-885356-64-1 | 19.95 | _____ |
| __ *Nurturing Your Newborn* | 1-885356-58-7 | 6.95 | _____ |
| — Workbook | 1-885356-61-7 | 2.00 | _____ |
| *Your Baby's First Year* | | | |
| — Paper | 1-932538-03-8 | 12.95 | _____ |
| — Hardcover | 1-932538-04-6 | 18.95 | _____ |
| — Workbook | 1-932538-05-4 | 2.50 | _____ |
| __ *BFY/NN Curriculum Notebook* | 1-885356-97-8 | 125.00 | _____ |
| **Four-video series — Your Baby's First Year** | | | |
| — **Nurturing Your Newborn** | 1-885356-86-2 | 69.95 | _____ |
| — **She's Much More Active** | 1-885356-87-0 | 69.95 | _____ |
| — **Leaving Baby Stage Behind** | 1-885356-88-9 | 69.95 | _____ |
| — **Keeping Your Baby Healthy** | 1-885356-89-7 | 69.95 | _____ |
| __ **All Four Videos — Baby's First Year Series** | | 195.00 | _____ |
| __ **Baby's First Year Board Game** | 1-885356-20-x | 29.95 | _____ |
| **Four-video series — Discipline from Birth to Three** | | | |
| — **Infants and Discipline** | 1-885356-82-x | 69.95 | _____ |
| — **He's Crawling — Help!** | 1-885356-83-8 | 69.95 | _____ |
| — **She's into Everything!** | 1-885356-84-6 | 69.95 | _____ |
| — **Your Busy Runabout** | 1-885356-85-4 | 69.95 | _____ |
| __ **All Four Videos — Discipline Birth to Three Series** | | 195.00 | _____ |

**SUB-TOTAL** (Carry over to top of next page) _____

**SUB-TOTAL FROM PREVIOUS PAGE** _____

# More Resources for Teen Parents:

*Discipline from Birth to Three*

| | | | |
|---|---|---|---|
| ___ | Paper | 1-932538-09-7 | 12.95 _____ |
| ___ | Hardcover | 1-932538-10-0 | 18.95 _____ |
| ___ | Workbook | 1-932538-11-9 | 2.50 _____ |
| ___ *Discipline Curriculum Notebook* | | 1-885356-99-4 | 125.00 _____ |

*The Challenge of Toddlers*

| | | | |
|---|---|---|---|
| ___ | Paper | 1-932538-06-2 | 12.95 _____ |
| ___ | Hardcover | 1-932538-07-0 | 18.95 _____ |
| ___ | Workbook | 1-932538-08-9 | 2.50 _____ |
| ___ *CT Curriculum Notebook* | | 1-885356-98-6 | 125.00 _____ |
| ___ **Challenge of Toddlers Bd. Game** | | 1-885356-56-0 | 29.95 _____ |

*Teen Dads: Rights, Responsibilities and Joys*

| | | | |
|---|---|---|---|
| ___ | Paper | 1-885356-68-4 | 12.95 _____ |
| ___ | Workbook | 1-885356-69-2 | 2.50 _____ |
| ___ *Teen Dads Curriculum Notebook* | | 1-995357-95-1 | 125.00 _____ |

**Following books are NOT included in Complete *Teens Parenting* Curriculum:**

| | | | |
|---|---|---|---|
| ___ *Do I Have a Daddy?* Hardcover | 0-885356-62-5 | 14.95 _____ |
| ___ *Pregnant? Adoption Is an Option* | 1-885356-08-0 | 11.95 _____ |
| ___ *Surviving Teen Pregnancy* | 1-885356-06-4 | 11.95 _____ |
| ___ *Teenage Couples: Caring, Commitment and Change* | | |
| ___ | 0-930934-93-8 | 9.95 _____ |
| ___ *Teenage Couples: Coping with Reality* | 0-930934-86-5 | 9.95 _____ |

**Novels by Marilyn Reynolds:**

| | | | |
|---|---|---|---|
| ___ *Love Rules* | 1-885356-76-5 | 9.95 _____ |
| ___ *If You Loved Me* | 1-885356-55-2 | 8.95 _____ |
| ___ *Baby Help* | 1-885356-27-7 | 8.95 _____ |
| ___ *But What About Me?* | 1-885356-10-2 | 8.95 _____ |
| ___ *Too Soon for Jeff* | 0-930934-91-1 | 8.95 _____ |
| ___ *Detour for Emmy* | 0-930934-76-8 | 8.95 _____ |
| ___ *Telling* | 1-885356-03-x | 8.95 _____ |
| ___ *Beyond Dreams* | 1-885356-00-5 | 8.95 _____ |

**TOTAL** _____

**Add postage: 10% of total—Min., $3.50; 15%, Canada** _____
**California residents add 7.75% sales tax** _____

**TOTAL** _____

Ask about quantity discounts, teacher, student guides.
Prepayment requested. School/library purchase orders accepted.
If not satisfied, return in 15 days for refund.

NAME _____

PHONE_____ Purchase Order #_____

ADDRESS _____